THE BREAKDOWN OF HIERARCHY

Communicating in the Evolving Workplace

Eugene Marlow

&

Patricia O'Connor Wilson

Routledge
Taylor & Francis Group

LONDON AND NEW YORK

First published by Butterworth-Heinemann

This edition published 2011 by Routledge
2 Park Square, Milton Park, Abingdon, Oxon OX14 4RN
711 Third Avenue, New York, NY 10017, USA

Routledge is an imprint of the Taylor & Francis Group, an informa business

Library of Congress Cataloging-in-Publication Data
Marlow, Eugene, 1943–
    The breakdown of hierarchy : communicating in the evolving workplace /
Eugene Marlow & Patricia O'Connor Wilson.
        p. cm.
    Includes bibliographical references and index.
    ISBN 0-7506-9746-6 (alk. paper)
    1. Communication in management. 2. Communication in organizations.
    3. Organizational change. 4. Business communication—Technological innovations.
    I. Wilson, Patricia O'Connor, 1964- . II. Title.
    HD30.3.M3666 1997
    658.4'5—dc21   96-39241
                                                                                    CIP

British Library Cataloguing-in-Publication Data
A catalogue record for this book is available from the British Library.

Epigraph

. . . everyone has to be able to talk with, work with, everyone else. . . .
The web of relations *is* the firm.

(Tom Peters, 1992, p. 181)

DEDICATION

To Jonathan and Samuel, who will inherit the
electronically mediated environment described in this book.

E.M.

To my parents, for paving the way.
To my siblings, for modeling myriad ways.
But mostly to my husband, for helping me create my way.

My love, respect, and gratitude to Grace D. & Cornelius J. O'Connor,
Neil O'Connor, Dick O'Connor, Ann Trauscht, Joe O'Connor,
Ginny Chiappetta, Michael O'Connor,
& Douglas A. Wilson.

P.O.W.

Related business titles
for Transforming Business

Beyond Strategic Vision: Effective Corporate Action with Hoshin Planning,
    Michael Cowley and Ellen Domb, 0-7506-9843-8

Beyond Time Management: Business with Purpose,
    Robert A. Wright, 0-7506-9799-7

The Breakdown of Hierarchy: Communicating in the Evolving Workplace,
    Eugene Marlow and Patricia O'Connor Wilson, 0-7056-9746-6

Business and the Feminine Principle: The Untapped Resource,
    Carol R. Frenier, 0-7506-9829-2

Cultivating Common Ground: Releasing the Power of Relationships at Work,
    Daniel S. Hanson, 0-7506-9832-2

*Fifth Generation Management: Co-creating Through Virtual Enterprising, Dynamic Teaming, and
    Knowledge Networking, Revised Edition,*
    Charles M. Savage, 0-7506-9701-6

Flight of the Phoenix: Soaring to Success in the 21st Century,
    John Whiteside and Sandra Egli, 0-7506-9798-9

Getting a Grip on Tomorrow: Your Guide to Survival and Success in the Changed World of Work,
    Mike Johnson, 0-7506-9758-X

Innovation Strategy for the Knowledge Economy: The Ken Awakening,
    Debra M. Amidon, 0-7506-9841-1

The Intelligence Advantage: Organizing for Complexity,
    Michael D. McMaster, 0-7506-9792-X

The Knowledge Evolution: Expanding Organizational Intelligence,
    Verna Allee, 0-7506-9842-X

Leadership in a Challenging World: A Sacred Journey,
    Barbara Shipka, 0-7506-9750-4

Leading from the Heart: Choosing Courage over Fear in the Workplace,
    Kay Gilley, 0-7506-9835-7

Learning to Read the Signs: Reclaiming Pragmatism in Business,
    F. Byron Nahser, 0-7506-9901-9

Marketing Plans That Work: Targeting Growth and Profitability,
    Malcolm H.B. McDonald and Warren J. Keegan, 0-7506-9828-4

A Place to Shine: Emerging from the Shadows at Work,
    Daniel S. Hanson, 0-7506-9738-5

Power Partnering: A Strategy for Business Excellence in the 21st Century,
    Sean Gadman, 0-7506-9809-8

Resources for the Knowledge-Based Economy Series

Knowledge Management and Organizational Design,
Paul S. Myers, 0-7506-9749-0

Knowledge Management Tools,
Rudy L. Ruggles, III, 0-7506-9849-7

Knowledge in Organizations,
Laurence Prusak, 0-7506-9718-0

The Strategic Management of Intellectual Capital,
David A. Klein, 0-7506-9850-0

Setting the PACE® in Product Development: A Guide to Product And Cycle-time Excellence,
Michael E. McGrath, 0-7506-9789-X

Time to Take Control: The Impact of Change on Corporate Computer Systems,
Tony Johnson, 0-7506-9863-2

The Transformation of Management,
Mike Davidson, 0-7506-9814-4

Who We Could Be at Work, Revised Edition,
Margaret A. Lulic, 0-7506-9739-3

Table of Contents

Preface

The *Wall Street Journal* has called change management "the biggest social issue of the next 20 years . . . as massive and wrenching as the Industrial Revolution." Consequently, we perceive the ability to manage change as the crucial business survival skill of this generation. What we view as inextricably part of this self-management is the intelligent and dynamic personal management of communication media (particularly electronic), content, and timing. Indeed, in Kanter, Stein, and Jick's *The Challenge of Organizational Change* (The Free Press, 1992) the authors highlight the effective personal communication skills of Motorola's Bob Galvin and General Electric's Jack Welch as key to their management of sweeping changes experienced by their respective companies.

The Breakdown of Hierarchy discusses the evolving role of communication within organizations as shaped by the major changes in technological, climatic, and organizational forces. The book also focuses on the key communication issues encountered by the various players in the new work environment—the "permanent" workforce (including executives and managers), contingent workers, and alliance partners, and discusses the impact of the various environmental changes on the deployment of effective communication.

This book attempts to present both the theoretical underpinnings (communication/organizational behavior theory) and practical approaches undertaken by managers to communicate with their internal publics. By discussing both the theory and practice of organizational communication, this book hopes to reach audiences in both profit and nonprofit organizational arenas. Corporate professionals in all functional areas will also benefit from this book as it centers on the salient communication issues confronting all professionals who work within the organizational environment.

By extension, professors and senior level undergraduates in the management, speech communications, human resources, organizational behavior, and public relations disciplines are potential audiences. Graduate business students in all disciplines are also potential audiences, as the book focuses on material not bound by functional specialty but on critical organizational and managerial issues.

This book's purpose is to create awareness for and heighten sensitivity to the major communication issues created by organizational, technological, and climatic change. The book also highlights the necessity of proactively employing strategic communication behaviors and considers the various changes driving the culture in which professionals find themselves. This book uses several techniques to deliver its content, including a combination of historical overviews, subject expert perspectives, technique descriptions, and practical applications.

The unique feature of this book is that it presents both the "hard" and "soft" sides of effective organizational communication by employing a combination of technological and psychological perspectives, which necessarily interrelate and ultimately complement each other. Finally, *The Breakdown of Hierarchy* merges theory and practice to provide a stronger foundation for the communication prescriptions outlined within it. While there are many books on both change management and communication techniques, to our knowledge no publication brings the technological and psychological perspectives together in one volume.

Portions of *The Breakdown of Hierarchy* have appeared elsewhere and serve as content springboards for the current volume. Sections of Chapter 2, "Electronic Media," originally appeared in *Electronic Public Relations* (Marlow, Eugene, Wadsworth Publishing, 1996). Parts of Chapter 3, "Electrovisual Media and the American Corporation," were first published in *Business Horizons*, a publication of the Indiana University Graduate School of Business, Bloomington, Indiana, in an article entitled "The Electrovisual Manager" (Marlow, Eugene, March-April 1994). This article serves as the intellectual genesis of the current volume. And, finally, material dealing with Linear Video in Chapter 7, "Harnessing the Power of Communication Technology," first appeared in *Corporate Television Programming*, (Marlow, Eugene, originally published by Knowledge Industry Publications, 1992).

EM
POW
1997

Chapter 1

Communications, Corporations, and Change

The Breakdown of Hierarchy: Communicating in the Evolving Workplace considers the impact of electronic media on the structure of American corporations in the second half of the 20th century and the resultant evolving relationship between managers and employees in the electrovisual environment. In effect, The Breakdown of Hierarchy explores the changes that have taken place, particularly since World War II, in the world of work because of electronic media and how organizations of all sizes can harness electronic media to meet the challenges of the evolving economic order.

In the last quarter century, explicit in any discussion of electronic media is the subject of change, a topic that has been at the center of much popular debate ever since the publication of Alvin Toffler's Future Shock in 1970. Yet should change concern us here? Is there a need for organizations to adapt their approach to communications—both interpersonal and mediated—in the years ahead?

In an address presented at Cornell University in 1973, the late Dr. Peter Goldmark (who developed, among other things, the long-playing record and color television) noted some of the changes that have marked human progress in the last 10,000 years:

> Ten thousand years ago the world population was no greater than New York
> City's today [in 1973 ten million people]. Too few people for the world, far too
> many for New York City. Yet, the human brain had the same size and
> capacity as it has today, namely, one-and-a-half liters. Human behavior,
> attitude, and man's general physical characteristics were no different 10,000

1

years ago than they are today. During the succeeding 9,800 years to the 19th century, all changes were extremely gradual.

Goldmark further points out that at the time America was discovered, the entire world population was only 50 million more people than there are in the United States today. Now, the world population is more than five billion people. During 9,000 of the past 10,000 years, the world population doubled every 2,000 years, whereas at today's rate it doubles every 35 years. The fastest a human could travel until the 19th century was roughly 25 miles per hour on or behind horses, while today humans travel at 25,000 miles per hour on the way to the moon. And the only explosives available throughout this period have no comparison to what has been unleashed since Hiroshima.

While noting the exponential rate of these curves during the last 150 years, however, Goldmark pinpointed " . . . an all important date still buried in relative tranquillity. This was the year 1455, when Gutenberg developed an important invention in communications, the movable type printing press. This event," stated Goldmark, "probably more than any other, contributed to the sudden increase in the rate of change in practically all aspects of our lives."

It was not until the 18th century that printing and book publishing came into general use. During the ensuing two centuries, the cumulative number of books published burgeoned from two million to fifty million titles, followed by an unprecedented upsurge in both scientific and techno-logical development. It was of course extremely difficult for the many indi-viduals dedicated to science before modern history to communicate their ideas to others. With the advent of the printing press, however, the new sci-entists were able to learn through books how to carry on from where their predecessors left off. The need to spend a lifetime creating something others may have already created was eliminated, and new discoveries, inventions, and theories burst forth at an unprecedented rate. The results were modern science, technology, and to a certain degree unplanned growth.

Combining the brief span of accomplishments by modern civilization into a single graph and plotting them on the scale of the past 10,000 years of human history, Goldmark obtained a curve, "which, within an incredibly short time, shoots up almost vertically and points to infinity." He went on to relate how " . . . this sudden and frightening increase in the rate at which changes occur is the measure of how rapidly we exhaust our natural resources and spoil our environment, and of how poorly we are planning ahead." Goldmark's perspective was directed at environmental issues. But his address can be equally applied to the impact of technology on society, on the one hand, and the need for planning, on the other.

Another perspective on technology's impact, particularly in this cen-tury, is offered by Grant Venn. In *Man, Education, and Manpower*, Venn points out how technology has changed the face of our society, with:

most work once done by muscle now being done by machines; food, fiber, and basic production now accounting for only a small part of the total labor force; the majority of the work force now being engaged in distribution and services; pollution of air, water, and cities creating social and economic problems; people who yesterday were economic assets today considered economic liabilities their sense of self-worth gone; fear of 'other kinds' of people on the rise; opportunity gaps between the uneducated and educated widening; the clash between 19th century technological thought and societal institutions escalating; and most institutions seeming to be strongly resistant to change.

The rapid progression of development and the increasing application of technology and automation are illustrated by the accelerating rate of change in several common areas. This nation and Western civilization in general (including Japan) have changed so much so fast in the last decade or two that the result cannot properly be looked at as a change of degree, but as an entirely new factor, a change of kind. The application of science and technology to the agricultural, industrial, and commercial institutions of our society has been so great as to create a revolution in the social, economic, and cultural activities of the country.

According to Venn, "In a technological society, especially in today's labor market, unemployment is more often the result of a lack of education and skill than of a shortage of job opportunities." However, with respect to education and job training, there is evidence of the dwindling ability of those who will become the employment targets for many corporations in the next five to fifteen years to write a simple sentence! Quite obviously, these social and economic factors have had, and will continue to have, a profound effect on our corporate institutions and will, in turn, affect the content, style, and manner of organizational communications.

Not surprisingly, many technological innovations in the last 158 years have been devices that are electronic in nature and have communications applications, devices that have enabled more and more people on a local level and international scale to share information—the telegraph, the phonograph, the telephone, the electric light, broadcast radio, broadcast television, cable television, high definition television, satellites, computers, lasers, electrostatic copiers, data voice linkage, coaxial cable, automation, miniaturization, holography, solid state electronics, mobile telephony, integrated circuits, media interfaces, microwave, feedback mechanisms, and translating machines.

Electronic communications technology has literally changed the way we do things, and how we respond to change, and has changed the way in which we look at the world and ourselves. We witness events as they happen—the Robert Kennedy assassination, the first moon walk, the Watergate hearings, the war in Vietnam, the Space Shuttle explosion, the Gulf War, and the O.J. Simpson car chase. Information and events are available to us all at the flip of a switch.

There is another message. We are becoming increasingly graphic and interactive in our communication of events, ideas, and information; there is a shift from print to pictures and electrovisual imagery. Moreover, while our demand for electronic communications resources is burgeoning, the cost of certain modes of communication is also increasing. Paper, quite obviously, has been the mainstay of our communications system for the last several hundred years. Yet there is evidence that using paper as a means of transporting information from one place to another is becoming too costly, as reflected by this and other countries' postal systems. Even 20 years ago, in 1976, for instance, it was reported that in the United States mail volume was decreasing, delivery points were increasing, and expenses were going up steadily. The United States was not the only country with postal problems. Lawrence Van Gelder, writing in *The New York Times*, noted that businessmen in many countries have complained about their respective postal services. Van Gelder informally rated the Chinese and Japanese systems as best, followed by the United States, Canada, France, West Germany, and India. Italy was considered to have one of the worst postal systems in the world, with insufficient delivery points, low pay for its workers, and mounting postal rates. One result, in Italy, as in the United States and elsewhere, was that members of the business community turned to private couriers for service.

While paper communication costs have risen, our ability to use information has transformed how we use our other resources. According to Myron Tribus and Edward C. McIrvine, "Today we know that it takes energy to obtain knowledge and that it takes information to harness energy." Tribus and McIrvine discuss the impact of information on humans, "A human operator, working with a fixed set of questions, can use a modern digital computer to amplify his abilities by a factor well in excess of 10 [to the sixth power], perhaps by a factor of 10 [to the 12th power]." On the other hand, they point out:

> It is worth observing that this great gap between the achieved and the achievable gives information technology a character different from that of materials technology or energy technology. In materials technology and energy technology scientists are accustomed to studying fundamental limitations and natural structures and engineers are accustomed to designing within a few orders of magnitude of these limitations.
>
> In information technology scientists find fundamental theorems not at all restrictive, and entrepreneurs discover that the freedom from constraints makes possible the construction of an almost totally new environment of information. Hence the advent of television programming, automatic telephone solicitation, computer-generated junk and mail and other artifacts of an information overload culture. In the case of material and energy nature often cries 'Halt!' to the changes wrought by technology. In the case of information man himself must issue the directives to ensure that technology is used for human betterment.

Jumping forward a couple of decades, Peter F. Drucker in *Managing in a Time of Great Change* (1995) brings the relationship between energy and information into a practical context when he observes, "Since 1900, the unit of labor needed for an additional unit of manufacturing output has been going down steadily at a compound rate of about 1 percent a year. Since the end of World War II, the unit of raw materials needed for an additional unit of manufacturing output has been decreasing at the same rate" (p. 41). Drucker goes on, "Since around 1950, the unit of energy needed for an additional unit of manufacturing output has also been going down steadily at that rate. But from the 1880s, since the telephone and Frederick Wilson Taylor's *Principles of Scientific Management*, the amounts of *information and knowledge* needed for each additional unit of output have been going up steadily at a compound rate of 1 percent a year—the rate at which businesses have added educated people to their payrolls" (p. 14).

T.C. Helvey, in *The Age of Information*, underscores Drucker's observation when he states, "Man will rely more and more on transmitted and decoded information, and his survival will not depend on his physical fitness, but on the quality of his communications system." Thus we posit: the survival of the organization in the marketplace of the future will depend increasingly on the quality of communications professionals, technology, and systems. Formal communications, managed by communications professionals, drawing on high technology and "systems" approaches, will make corporations more flexible and more responsive to internal and external needs.

As the next chapter will discuss, we have already seen how personal values stressing the importance of the individual and fulfillment conflict with a technologically oriented society that has been dominated by the pyramid, bureaucratic style of too many of today's institutions. As a result, even more than today, the person-organization interface will be a mass of contradictions. These contradictions will create stress for the organization in its treatment of employees. Changing employee attitudes toward work, loyalty to the corporation, and their rights and obligations will also force changes in internal communications systems. To function effectively, organizations will have to listen to the aspirations and needs of the individuals within the organization. And this listening and understanding will be a continuous process because of the continuing and accelerating rate of change. Top management will particularly discover that lower management and other employees find inadequate jobs and motivational systems designed for a stereotype imprinted out of memories of a fading past.

Organizational survival will depend on effective communications to achieve consonance of employee and organization goals. New communications tools will impact heavily on consumer purchasing methods and, therefore, on marketing methods. The home communication data center, with its roots in personal computers, multichannel cable TV systems, and response mechanisms, will permit examination, analysis, and ordering of goods from home. Such services will, presumably, be appreciated by the physically handicapped, the elderly, the frenetically busy, and those who just hate to shop! But before we close down traditional retailing, however, let us remember that many consumers prefer to make their purchases in stores after seeing, hearing, touching, smelling, and tasting the goods; sampling the service; or having a real, live salesperson convince them. Futurists frequently forget that people enjoy going shopping, that is, they enjoy the temporary socializing gained from shopping in the flesh. Marketing efforts will be forced to reflect the greater diversity in buying sites; point-of-purchase will still exist, but in a multitude of forms.

Time will also be a crucial factor in communications' impact on organizational management of marketing activities. Better access to central data banks, demographic data, information on changing values and tastes, and marketing performance reports will enable organizations using management sciences to adapt quickly to changing markets. Speaking at a meeting of the American College Public Relations Association, Scott M. Cutlip, former Dean of the University of Georgia, pointed out some of the problems for public relations practitioners resulting from this technological and information access explosion: the necessity to interact with (1) a public having more power in terms of information availability; (2) to face a public backed by publicly funded consumer institutes; (3) to face a disbelieving public that is becoming increasingly segmented into smaller, more selective audiences; and (4) to face a public influenced and disturbed by a major energy and environmental crisis.

Cutlip also stated that these portents of the future will require that public relations people (1) reorient to the electronic media; (2) develop tools to better identify problems and publics, pretest message and media, and post test to identify and measure attitude change; (3) be able to more accurately measure the impact of communications on individuals, groups, or societies; (4) develop a more adequate "early warning" radar system providing indicators of social behavior; and (5) serve as full-range communications consultants and advisors to all divisions of their organization, that is, technology will continue to have an impact on the management and organization of the corporation.

Warren G. Bennis and Phillip E. Slater, in *The Temporary Society*, proposed that the organization of the future will be "project oriented" rather than function oriented. That is, because the marketing environment will be in a constant state of change, vested functional interests (production, finance, sales, personnel) might hamper organizational adjustments to the visibly evolving environment. The free-form, diversified companies of the 1960s, such as LTV and the Rexall Drug and Chemical Company, were forerunners of the project-oriented company. Following Rexall's organizational example, financial planning was centralized and marketing decentralized. Divisions were allowed greater autonomy and flexibility with respect to any aspect of the profitability of the product without having to wait for a decision from top management. The implications of technological change and product obsolescence present a situation in which the various functions of a corporation must work closer together if the firm is to survive, and they must be provided with accurate, succinct, and timely information. Communications effectiveness throughout the corporation will thus become imperative for survival. Top management must devise ways of training and retraining management staff as markets shift, products die, new products develop, and employee and customer attitudes change. But will conventional approaches and techniques solve the information gap? Or, to put it another way, how will managerial obsolescence be averted?

It follows there is a need for systems-oriented managers who must have the ability to conceptualize the organization as a system and see that system within the external marketing system. As Anne P. Carter has pointed out, ". . . a principal consequence of technological change [is that] the diverse major industries in the United States economy tend to become interlocked in increasing interdependence. In the job market there is declining demand for people in the 'productive' functions, as traditionally defined, and increasing demand for people who can contribute to the coordinating and integrating functions required by the larger and more complex system." Peter Drucker, in *The Age of Discontinuity*, stated that management performance will be a criterion for success and reward. Drucker also proposed that the ability to perform a job will be based less on skills acquired in school or through experience than on acquired knowledge, that is, information acquired through an effective and efficient communication system. Yet how will the constantly evolving knowledge be presented and acquired?

Communication technology will affect all activities of the corporation—advertising, marketing, public relations, and internal organizational communications. The cost-effective use of communications within and without the corporation to (1) create understanding and (2) make knowledge more productive provides the corporation with a key to survival. Modern communications and information theory is over 60 years old, but what is lacking is the effective and efficient use of modern communications media to create understanding and make knowledge more productive. There are too many instances of failure to understand communications as a discipline and communication technology as tools.

Thus, while organizations spend millions on training devices, video production hardware, art departments, writers, talent, and engineers, much of the investment is wasted due to a lack of a systematic communications needs analysis of the organization as a total entity and needs analysis of communications projects as they occur. Since systems approaches are being used elsewhere in the organization with accounting, production, and marketing, why not also with communications? Perhaps it is because our economic system has made it unattractive for organizations to change unless management perceives change as either necessary for survival or clearly cost effective. We have already discussed the former; let us not ignore the latter.

Communications in the organization is begging for a systems approach—at the very least, a team approach. Yet organizationally, communications activities have been scattered over many divisions within the organization (in public relations, training, personnel, marketing, and advertising, to name but a few). Thus, organizations are unable to take full advantage of "coordinated communications" under one roof. While it is possible to improve the effectiveness of organizational communication without restructuring it, and the discussions in the following chapters do not require that you first redesign the organization chart, the advantages of coordinated communication operations should not be treated lightly. Let us now briefly review the development of electronic media (Chapter 2) and then examine how electronic communications technologies have altered the shape of American corporations, particularly the role of middle managers (Chapter 3).

Chapter 2

Electronic Media

Sudden Impact or Business as Usual?

Electronic technologies have acted true to Marshall McLuhan's (1964) contention that "Once a new technology comes into a social milieu it cannot cease to permeate that milieu until every institution is saturated" (p. 177). In recent times it appears these technologies have also dramatically impacted the "shape" of American corporations and institutions. The consistent message of electronic media over time is an evolution from media that can reach many people at one time (such as broadcast radio and television) to media that can reach a few people at any time (such as CD-ROM, the Internet, and the World Wide Web). In effect, as the 20th century has progressed, electronic communications media have become more accessible to more people on a global scale. Geographic, physical, and political boundaries have been transcended. Time, similarly, has been transcended. The dissemination of news, for example, is no longer time dependent. It can be accessed on a 24-hour-a-day basis. A corollary to this is that over time electronic communications media have moved from linear (one-way communication) to interactive (two-way communication).

It is important to understand the electronic media context in which so much internal employee and management communications takes place. Further, in order to make effective and efficient use of electronic media, it is wise to understand how they developed and what they can do.

The First Electronic Medium: The Telegraph

In early 1838 Samuel Finley Breese Morse—artist, daguerrotypist, a so-called American Leonardo—gave a series of public demonstrations of the first practical electromagnetic telegraph (Czitrom, 1982, pp. 4–5). In 1844, after receiving a thirty-thousand dollar grant to construct a telegraph line between Baltimore and Washington D.C. in the previous the year, Morse finally opened the nation's first commercial telegraph line on May 24 with the now famous query, "What hath God wrought?" (pp. 5–6). On that day the electronic communications age was born.

The commercial development of the telegraph—the precursor of all electronic media—occurs at almost the same time as the conceptualization of the modern computer and digital technology. Bill Gates, Chairman and Chief Executive Officer of the Microsoft Corporation, observes in *The Road Ahead*:

> Charles Babbage was a professor of mathematics at Cambridge University who conceived the possibility of a mechanical device that would be able to perform a string of related calculations. As early as the 1830s, he was drawn to the idea that information could be manipulated by a machine if the information could be converted into numbers first. The steam-powered machine Babbage envisioned would use pegs, toothed wheels, cylinders, and other mechanical parts, the apparatus of the then-new Industrial Age. Babbage believed his "Analytical Engine" would be used to take the drudgery and inaccuracy out of calculating.
>
> (Gates, 1995, p. 22.)

The Telephone and the Telephone Company

AT&T was incorporated in 1885 but traces its lineage to Alexander Graham Bell and his invention of the telephone in 1876. As parent company of the former Bell System, AT&T's primary mission was to provide universal telephone service—service to virtually everyone in the United States. It also provided international long distance service. The Bell System was dissolved at the end of 1983 with AT&T's divestiture of the Bell telephone companies (webmaster@att.com).

In 1927 AT&T inaugurated commercial transatlantic telephone service to London using two-way radio. Initially, these calls cost $75 each (for five minutes). Service spread to other countries, both via London and through direct radio links. Radio-telephone service to Hawaii began in 1931, and to Tokyo in 1934. Telephone service via available radio technology was far from ideal—it was subject to fading and interference, and had strictly limited capacity. In 1956, service to Europe moved to the first transatlantic submarine telephone cable, TAT-1. Transpacific cable service began in 1964. (sheldon@library.att.com).

Radio

Seventy-eight years after the commercial introduction of the telegraph, the basis for modern network broadcasting was created in the United States by the American Telephone & Telegraph Company. In February 1922 the company proposed that 38 radio broadcasting stations be linked by AT&T long distance telephone lines. The stations would each be charged a fee by AT&T and would be encouraged, in turn, to sell for commercial purposes the air time they had available. The commercial aspects of the proposal were condemned by many in the press, some of whom may have been anticipating unwanted competition for advertisers' dollars (Marlow and Secunda, 1991, pp. 25–26).

In 1922, AT&T opened radio station WEAF in New York based on a novel concept, toll broadcasting. AT&T saw WEAF's service as parallel to telephone service. The company would provide no programs, only facilities. Whomever wished to address a message to the radio audience would pay a toll or fee to use the station. It was to be a kind of telephone booth of the air. Of course, the telephone company soon found that it had to provide programming on a sustaining (unsponsored) basis when there were no messages (Smith, 1985, p. 20).

On August 28, 1922 at 5:00 p.m. WEAF aired its first toll broadcast. A Mr. Blackwell of the Queensboro Corporation spoke for ten minutes about Hawthorne Court, a condominium in the Jackson Heights section of Long Island, New York. The toll was $50. The first commercial had been broadcast (p. 20). AT&T was ultimately pressured by the federal government to divest itself of its radio network, which had rapidly grown to 26 stations. In 1926 the stations were sold to RCA, which formed a subsidiary, NBC, to operate the chain. NBC's first president was David Sarnoff (Marlow and Secunda, 1991, p. 26). By 1950, 95 percent of all American families owned a radio (p. 27). In 1994, there were more than 11,000 AM and FM radio stations in the United States. The average U.S. household has 5.6 radio receivers, totaling about 576,500,000. Radio reaches 96 percent of persons 12 years and older weekly (National Association of Broadcasters, 1994, p. 34).

Broadcast Television Networks

Commercial television broadcasting began in a limited way in 1941 but was temporarily abandoned at the start of World War II. Plans to launch the new medium in the United States were resumed following the end of hostilities in 1945. Less than a year later television broadcasting in America began (Marlow and Secunda, 1991, p. 29). Only 6,000 television sets were sold to Americans in 1946. The following year the number jumped to 179,000. Four networks emerged to provide programming—NBC, CBS, DuMont, and ABC. In 1948, generally regarded as the year when commercial broadcast television emerged as a major mass medium in the United States, only 17 stations were broadcasting. Within a year there were 51 (p. 30). Over 1,100 television stations broadcast commercially sponsored programming to over 98 million television households (Adweek Magazines, 1994, p. 20).

Cable Television

According to some accounts, the first cable television system was constructed in Astoria, Oregon in 1949 by the owner of a local radio station (Hollowell, 1980, p. 3.). In 1972 the Federal Communications Commission launched a cable access experiment requiring cable system operators, in certain locations, to provide the public sector with access channels and five minutes of free production time (p. 102). From these modest beginnings, various technological developments, not the least of which is satellite technology, have spawned a formidable entertainment and information delivery system—cable television.

The cable television industry, as of the end of 1995, was a $25.3 billion industry (basic and pay revenues), taking in an additional $5.3 billion in advertising revenues (National Cable Television Association, 1995, pp. 8, 9). In 1995 there were 11,218 cable television systems in communities throughout the United States. This compares with only 2,490 in 1970! These cable television systems boasted between 57 and 60 million subscribers (depending on whether you read A.C. Nielsen Co. or Paul Kagan Associates). This compares with the 94+ million television households in the United States. In effect, cable television (basic and/or pay) reaches between 62 and 64 percent of the television viewing households in America (p. 1-A).

Videotape and Organizational Video Networks

At the National Association of Radio and Television Broadcasters (NARTB) Show in Chicago in April 1956, Ampex introduced a commercially viable 900-pound quadraplex videotape recorder using 2-inch wide tape manufactured by 3M. It sold initially for $75,000 per unit and functioned only in black and white (Marlow and Secunda, 1991, p. 16). Just a few years later, by the late 1950s, a handful of so-called nonbroadcast organizations, including the United States Air Force, the University of Texas, Buick, and Ford, had adopted the videotape medium for a variety of programming purposes (pp. 85–86). In 1971 the Sony Corporation introduced the first 3/4–inch U-Matic videocassette to the American market; in 1975, they introduced the 1/2–inch Betamax format (p. 19). In the 1990s, thousands of corporate, medical, legal, educational, religious, and governmental organizations use linear videotape technology for a wide variety of internal and external communications applications. Clearly, in 40+ years the use of videotape has gone far beyond original expectations in broadcast and nonbroadcast contexts.

In the early era of video a handful of individuals and organizations enthusiastically adopted the medium, while most others either could not afford it or were askance to try it. And even with the advent of the video-cassette in the 1970s, there was still resistance to the medium in the corporate world, at least. It has taken decades for the medium to become truly part of the "communications" landscape. Today there seems to be no organization that does not take the VCR for granted. Videotape is now everywhere. According to D/J Brush Associates (LaGrangeville, New York), the growth rate for the nonbroadcast video market in the 1980s was in excess of 30 percent. Today the industry is predicted to grow approximately by 15 percent.

It is probable that linear videotape reached its zenith in the late 1980s as an electrovisual technology, at least in a nonbroadcast context. Over the next decade or so, this technology, which gave birth to a cornucopia of management communications channels, will probably slowly, but surely, give way to other electrovisual technologies, such as the CD-ROM, and, ultimately, an integrated system that combines the computer with a CD, plus desktop teleconferencing capability.

Interactive Videodisc

From the perspective of the 1990s it is easy to make the assumption that multimedia technology had interactive videodisc technology—first commercially introduced in 1978—as its technological precursor. But as Emmy-award winning engineer Mark Schubin points out in "An Overview and History of Video Disc Technologies," ". . . the three major forms of television storage—discs, magnetic tape, and film—all had their origins in . . . 1927" (Schubin, 1980, p. 7). Schubin recounts how a means of television signal storage was found in a patent application filed by Boris Rtcheouloff on January 4, 1927 in Britain. His proposal would have applied the magnetic recording techniques developed by Valdemar Poulsen at the end of the last century to television (p. 8). Schubin also relates how two scientists—R.V.L. Hartley and H.E. Ives of Electrical Research Products—felt that both the lighting problem and the dim, tiny image problem of very early television might be solved by interposing film at the imaging and display points. On September 14, 1927, they publicly announced their method of intermediate film television (p. 8). The third 1927 proposal for video recording was put forth by John Logie Baird, generally considered the first person to achieve recognizable television pictures. Baird's system was called Phonovision (p. 9).

Almost thirty years later, in April 1956 at the National Association of Radio and Television Broadcasters (NARTB) Show in Chicago, Ampex introduced a commercially viable 900-pound quadraplex videotape recorder using 2-inch wide tape manufactured by 3M. This television storage technology was partly based on the pioneering work of the Germans who during World War II had developed audio magnetic recording. Nine years later, Magnetic Video Recording ". . . provided a magnetic disc for video recording that provided stop action and instant replay for a CBS football pickup on July 8, 1965" (Schubin, p. 13). (It is interesting to note that CBS was also the first broadcaster to purchase the Ampex manufactured Quadraplex videotape recording machines.)

Thirteen years later, in 1978, Philips and MCA introduced the first interactive multimedia format—the analog laser videodisc—to the North American market (Banet, 1992, p. 11). The laserdisc provided a full-screen, full-motion video, two tracks of good audio, and up to 108,000 still color images. In addition to Philips and MCA, IBM and Pioneer in various combinations (e.g., DiscoVision) brought out laserdisc players that could be interfaced with the microcomputers of the day, as well as players that were manufactured with internal microprocessors. As Bernard Banet points out, "These made it possible to link the computer's text files, structured databases, computer graphics, and logic with the laser discs' audiovisual sights and sound" (p. 11).

Multimedia

While there are certainly similarities between interactive videodisc and multimedia, multimedia is distinct from interactive videodisc. Robert E. Bergman and Thomas V. Moore (1990), writing in *Managing Interactive Video/Multimedia Projects*, make the following observation: "For several years, the videodisc was the only source of motion video segments that could be accessed rapidly enough to support effective interactivity. Hence, the term applied to these applications came to be 'interactive videodisc,' or more commonly, 'IVD.' Recently, however, digital technology has made it possible to provide motion video using other devices, especially the small optical discs called CD-ROM" (p. 5).

The adoption of interactive multimedia technology, particularly CD-ROM, is growing in both nonprofit and for-profit organizations. Microsoft points to a range of factors fueling this growth, including:

> More powerful microprocessors capable of handling large, complex files needed for multimedia information.
>
> Advances in computer software, from new graphical user interfaces to object-oriented programming, that make electronic systems faster, easier, and more efficient.
>
> Emerging standards around digital audio, video, and multimedia systems.
>
> (*Microsoft Backgrounder*, February 1993, p. 2.)

Satellites and Teleconferencing

In 1945 Arthur C. Clark (best known for his short story upon which the movie *2001: A Space Odyssey* is based) suggested in the British academic journal *Wireless World* the concept of a geosynchronous satellite positioned 22,300 miles above the equator as the perfect platform for television broadcasting (Rogers, 1986, p. 58). In 1957 Russia launched Sputnik, the first space satellite (p. 25). Almost 40 years later, according to the International Teleconferencing Association (ITCA), a clearinghouse for the teleconferencing industry, teleconferencing in its various forms is expected to post revenues that will break the $4.8 billion mark in 1996. This compares with the $4 billion in total revenues in 1995 and the 1991 revenues of $1.43 billion. In effect, the teleconferencing business will have more than tripled in six years! (International Teleconferencing Association, News Release, May 21, 1996; June 14, 1993.)

Computers and LANs

In 1946 the first electronic calculator, the Electronic Numerical Integrator and Calculator, ENIAC for short, with 70,000 resistors and 17,000 vacuum tubes (weighing 30 tons) was developed at the Moore School of Electrical Engineering in the University of Pennsylvania (Forester, 1987, p. 17). The device was developed by a group of mathematicians led by J. Presper Eckert and John Mauchly. Its purpose, Bill Gates reports, ". . . was to speed up the calculations for artillery-aiming tables" (Gates, 1995, p. 26). Needless to say, this is not the first time a technology was developed whose initial purpose evolved into something quite different. In 1971 the microprocessor, a computer-control unit on a semiconductor chip, was invented by Ted Hoff at Intel Corporation, a Silicon Valley microelectronics company (Rogers, 1986, p. 25).

Over 20 years later personal computers and computer networks are rampant in tens of thousands of organizations. Today there are more than 100 million computers in the world whose purpose is to manipulate information (Gates, 1995, p. 5), and computer chips now show up in engines, watches, antilock brakes, facsimile machines, elevators, gasoline pumps, cameras, thermostats, treadmills, vending machines, burglar alarms, and even talking greeting cards (Gates, 1995, p. 3). Lawrence G. Tesler, writing in the September 1991 issue of *Scientific American* ("Network Computing in the 1990s") provides a graph correlating the relative cost of computation from 1950 into the 1990s. His graph indicates that computing cost has been halved approximately every three years with respect to the most powerful commercial machines, starting with the IBM 650 to the more recent CRAY Y-MP/864 (p. 88).

Paralleling the drop in computing cost is the capacity of a computer chip. Bill Gates reports:

In 1965, Gordon Moore, who later cofounded Intel with Bob Noyce, predicted that the capacity of a computer chip would double every year. He said this on the basis of having examined the price/performance ratio of computer chips over the previous three years and projecting it forward. In truth, Moore didn't believe that this rate of improvement would last long. But ten years later, his forecast proved true, and he then predicted the capacity would double every two years. To this day his predictions have held up, and the average—a doubling every eighteen months—is referred to among engineers as Moore's law.

(Gates, 1995, pp. 31–32.)

Thomas W. Malone and John F. Rockart, both of the Massachusetts Institute of Technology, also writing in the September 1991 issue of *Scientific American* ("Computers, Networks and the Corporation") point to the effects of computers and computer networks. They say, "The revolution underway today will be driven not by changes in production but by changes in coordination" (p. 128). Further on they comment, "By dramatically reducing the costs of coordination and increasing its speed and quality, these new technologies will enable people to coordinate more effectively, to do much more coordination and to form new, coordination-intensive business structures" (p. 128).

E-mail

E-mail would not exist without computers, LANs, or a burgeoning telecommunications system. As Jim Manzi, former CEO of the Lotus Development Corporation, pointed out in a keynote speech to the Electronic Messaging Association (EMA, May 8, 1995), electronic messaging has gone through several stages of development in the last 10 to 15 years:

"The first was early e-mail, or simple text that was the inheritance of 5-bit Telex and became 7-bit ASCII. The second was simple text with file and simple object attachments . . . The third stage was rich text with attachments—with the development of multiple fonts and colors. The fourth stage, which has emerged today, is complex, replicated objects with multiple links."

Manzi argues that ". . . this fourth stage in messaging is very close to what we mean by groupware. In fact, I want to go even further and argue that groupware—which I realize is still a very slippery and ill-defined term—is not really a product category that builds upon messaging or is separate from it. It is really the natural evolution of messaging and subsumes it."

E-mail in its various forms has become a multibillion business. The EMA predicts a $61 billion market by the year 2000. In a October 20, 1995 report, the EMA released the preliminary results of its 1995 Market Research Study focusing on the economic outlook for the electronic messaging industry (the complete study became available in early 1996). Conducted by the New York-based research company, Wilkofsky/Gruen & Associates, the study estimates the size of the messaging market with a quantifiable, economically defensible estimate of the dollar value of each major segment of the U.S. and Canadian markets.

The base component of the study is designed to estimate the number of users and size of the electronic mail market segment of the larger electronic messaging market. Through a combination of primary and secondary research, the imputed value of electronic mail in the workplace in 1994 was $12.7 billion and $0.5 billion at home, totaling $13.2 billion. Based upon the economic analysis of the demand for electronic mail and a variety of market factors, the growth to the year 2000 is projected at $61.3 billion.

The Internet

The development of on-line information services, such as CompuServe, Prodigy, and America On-Line, among others, has its probable beginnings with the Internet. What began as a United Department of Defense communications network in 1968 has now broadened to a worldwide network . . . and advertising, marketing, public relations, and organizational communications professionals are finding applications for it. According to John Perry Barlow writing in *Netguide*, "When it was first patched together in 1968, DARPANET, as it was then called, connected machines in the computer-science departments of seven universities at speeds that were geologically deliberate by today's standards" (*Netguide*, p. xvi).

Today, the Internet is a worldwide network linking thousands of computers and millions of people. The Internet has grown far beyond its government and university roots to include commercial institutions and individual users around the world. The Internet has become a network of more than 15,000 networks connecting over 38 million people. An additional 150,000 connect each month for the first time. By 1998 it is projected that 100 million people will be using the Internet (Angell and Heslop, 1994, p. 3), and 200 million by the end of the decade (Lewis, 1995, p. C15).

Unlike traditional on-line commercial services, in which one computer system serves a single dedicated group of people, the Internet connects computers together using standard sets of hardware and software worldwide. Once connected, computers can then exchange electronic mail and files, share public "news" discussions, search for information, and remotely access other archives and information services worldwide. A user can find many organizations on the Internet, such as computer companies and other high-tech corporations; most government agencies, such as the Defense Department, NASA, EPA, the Library of Congress, the White House, and the House of Representatives; and nearly all universities. Building on this base, many commercial companies and media organizations are joining the Internet to distribute information, provide customer support, and take product orders. Individuals are tapping into Internet resources to conduct research and keep in touch with people around the country and the world with high-speed links that connect Asia, Latin America, Africa, and all of Europe.

According to Washington, D.C.-based netResults, "The futuristic 'information superhighway' touted by Al Gore, John Malone, Bill Gates, and the Internet have a great deal in common. Both are interactive, which means a consumer can both receive and send information. Both rely on sophisticated electronic networks that can send enormous packets of information, at the speed of light, from one corner of the globe to the other. Both represent the future for business in the 21st century. The difference, though, is that the 'information superhighway' is a vision, a plan, a concept. The Internet is here today and will most certainly be incorporated into the 'superhighway' of the future. The advent of personal computers is clearly a moving force in the evolution of on-line service as well as software.

The *net* is often called the electronic highway or the information highway. It is also called *cyberspace*, a term coined by science-fiction writer and novelist William Gibson in his 1984 book *Neuromancer*:

> Cyberspace. A consensual hallucination experienced daily by billions of legitimate operators, in every nation, by children being taught mathematical concepts . . . A graphic representation of data abstracted from the banks of every computer in the human system. Unthinkable complexity. Lines of light ranged in the nonspace of the mind, clusters and constellations of data. Like city lights receding.
>
> (Rheingold, 1991, p. 16.)

Gibson's description of cyberspace as "lines of light" is not unlike the early descriptions of Samuel B. Morse's telegraph as "lightning lines." (Czitrom, 1982, chap. 1). Further, as Czitrom points out, the concept of communication in terms of light can be found in the Bible (Job 38:35): "Canst thou send lightnings, that they may go, and say unto thee, Here we are?" Czitrom elaborates, "This Biblical quotation, one of the impossibilities enumerated to convince Job of his ignorance and weakness, frequently prefaced nineteenth-century writing on the telegraph" (p. 9). Czitrom also states, "Before the telegraph there existed no separation between transportation and communication. Information traveled only as fast as the messenger who carried it. The telegraph dissolved that unity and quickly spread across the land to form the first of the great communication networks" (p. 3). To this we can add that the Internet—a.k.a. the net, cyberspace, the information superhighway—is the latest of the "great communication networks" linking millions of people around the globe.

A major relatively recent development in the exponential growth of the Internet is the World Wide Web (WWW). The Web began in March 1989, when Tim Berners-Lee of CERN (the European Laboratory for Particle Physics located in Geneva, Switzerland, a collective of European high-energy physics researchers) proposed the project to be used as a means of transporting research and ideas effectively throughout the organization. Effective communications was a goal of CERN for many years, as its members were located in a number of countries. The goal of the project is to build a distributed hypermedia system. The purpose of this system is to allow the exchange of information across the Internet in the form of hypertext documents.

Hypertext is text with pointers to other text, allowing the user to *branch-off* to another document for more information on a given topic, and then return to the same location in the original document with ease. To access the Web, the user runs a *client* on their computer, which accesses a WWW server running on another computer. In WWW terms the client is called a *browser*. The browser reads and retrieves documents from WWW *servers*.

Information providers establish WWW servers for use by a network user with WWW browsers. The browsers can, in addition, access files by FTP, gopher, and an ever-increasing range of other methods. Browsers are available for many computer platforms. WWW browsers and servers also deliver hypermedia documents to network users. Hypermedia is a superset of hypertext; it is any medium with pointers to other media. This means that browsers are able to display images, sound, or animations in addition to text.

Months after CERN's original proposal, the National Center for Supercomputing Applications (NCSA) began a project to create an interface to the World Wide Web. One of NCSA's missions is to aid the scientific research community by producing widely available, noncommercial software. Another of its goals is to investigate new research technologies in the hope that commercial interests will be able to profit from them. In these ways, the Web project was quite appropriate. The NCSA's Software Design Group began work on a versatile, multiplatform interface to the World Wide Web and called it *Mosaic*. In the first half of 1993, the first version of NCSA's Web browser was made available to the Internet community. Because earlier beta versions were distributed, Mosaic had developed a strong yet small following by the time it was officially released. Because of the number of traditional services it could handle, and due to its easy, point-and-click hypermedia interface, Mosaic soon became the most popular interface to the Web. However, by 1995 Netscape had eclipsed all other Web browsers and captured at least 75 percent of the market. By spring 1996 its dominance as *the* browser had risen to over 90 percent.

There is other evidence that the Internet is growing in prevalence, according to various surveys, as follows:

FIND/SVP: In January 1996 published the "American Internet User Survey," stating that, "9.5 million Americans now use the Internet, including 8.4 million adults and 1.1 million children under 18, who tap into it from the workplace, school, and homes."

Gartner Group Internet Strategies Section: In January 1996 forecasted that there will be over 150 million Internet users by 1998.

GVU Web User Surveys: The Fifth User Survey, published in June 1996, was conducted from April 10 to May 10, 1996. Findings include: "Average age has risen again slightly to 33.0 years old. The gender ratio continues to become more balanced, with 31.5% reporting being female, compared to 29.3% for the Fourth survey."

Internet Domain Survey carried out by Network Wizards: In January 1996 survey found that there were 9,472,000 host computers, up from 6,642,000 in July 1995. Observations include: "No one has any clue how many users there are, but most people would agree that there is at least one user per host."

Jupiter Communications: In April 1996 survey predicted that total on-line households in the United States will reach 35 million by the year 2000 (34 percent of all U.S. households).

Killen & Associates: Internet: In May 1996 Global Penetration and Forecast 2000 survey results estimated that at the beginning of 1996 there were 30 million Internet users worldwide. Stated, "In early 1996, 170 countries were connected to the Internet. By 2000, as many as 250 million people worldwide will have access to the Internet, through almost 96 million host computers."

Manning, Selvage & Lee (MS&L): MS&L's Corporate Cyber-Dash Survey found that while many companies have their own websites, company communicators are not using the Web very much yet. Findings include that 66 percent of 500 corporate communicators questioned in the United States and Europe had access to the Internet; however, 80 percent did not consider it an important communications tool. On the bright side, respondents felt that by the year 2000 there would be a fourfold or higher increase in the importance of the Internet with regard to reaching their respective target audiences. The survey found that e-mail is very popular, with company communicators spending an average of 1.19 hours a day using it.

Project 2000: April 1996 study, entitled: "Internet Use in the United States: 1995 Baseline Estimates and Preliminary Market Segments." Estimates that, "28.8 million people in the United States 16 and over have potential or actual access to the Internet, 16.4 million people use the Internet, 11.5 million people use the Web, and 1.51 million people have used the Web to purchase something."

Summary

The electronic media age began with the telegraph in the late 1830s (a technology using a series of dots and dashes to represent letters of the alphabet—itself a digitization of sounds of speech)—moved to linear, noninteractive technologies in the early 1920s (such as broadcast radio, broadcast and cable television, and videotape), and moved on to interactive technologies (such as multimedia, the Internet, and the World Wide Web) in the mid-1990s. The instant that the telegraph was commercially applied, the concept of *information access* was changed forever. Now information could be *messengered* at the speed of light. Physical boundaries (and subsequently political ones as well) were transcended. Leaping forward to the present day, the meaning of the Internet is that anyone with a computer, modem, telephone line, telecommunications software, and an Internet access provider can communicate with anyone, anywhere in the world, at any time, with comparable hardware and software. The Internet user can also access information in seconds without having to go through layers of clerks to get to the information, that is, presuming the information is on-line. Increasingly more and more information is accessible via the Internet on a global scale.

The meaning of electronic media since 1838 is that it is part of the inexorable march towards the externalization and extension of our senses on a global scale. In the proverbial beginning, the old man sat around the campfire telling the stories of the tribe. Everyone in earshot was part of the village communication system. Today, our campfire is electronic and global—we have realized the global village (some even call it the global theater!). In effect, humans (as a species) are in the process of externalizing their senses and extending their ability to communicate at increasingly greater distances in shorter and shorter time spans. It is a matter of time before the Internet as a communication system can also be used habitually for audio as well as visual communication. And it will be portable.

The meaning of electronic media for the for-profit and not-for-profit organizational manager and executive is that organizations of all kinds are inexorably moving towards the organization of work around the flow of information. As Drucker states in *Managing in a Time of Great Change* (1995):

> . . . it is a safe prediction that in the next fifty years, schools and universities
> will change more and more drastically than they have since they assumed
> their present form more than three hundred years ago, when they reorganized
> themselves around the printed book. What will force these changes is in part
> new technology; in part the demands of a knowledge-based society in which
> organized learning must become a lifelong process for knowledge workers;
> and in part new theory about how human beings learn (p. 79).

In other words, the impact of electronic media is not merely in the creation of new markets (such as the home video market with the development of the Beta and later the VHS videotape formats). Electronic media have had and will continue to engender the inexorable shift of organizations to an organizational structure that has *information* and ultimately *knowledge* as its focus.

Lest the reader come away with the impression that all this description is yet another example of how "new media" are creating an "information revolution," we suggest a pause here. On the contrary, electronic media in and of themselves are not revolutionary—they are but extensions and expansions of technological developments that were first commercially introduced in the early part of the last century. Moreover, if the reader takes the time to explore each electronic medium, he or she will find that (as with all technologies) antecedents abound. For example, humans have dreamt of flying for many centuries, but controlled flight was not possible until the 20th century. Further, there are always those (the so-called news media included) who "predict" that new media will "revolutionize" the world we live in. On the contrary, new media have not revolutionized the world we live in, rather they have expanded our access to the world while at the same time contracting the time it takes to experience it.

New media have not taken over the world, nor will they. If new media is about to or is in the process of taking over the world, why then are we still talking to each other (in person and over the phone), attending more entertainment and sports events, writing to each other (there is an ostensible increase in the volume of handwritten notes), writing books, listening to the radio, making more home movies than ever, publishing more magazines than ever, creating more television channels than ever, traveling more than ever, doing more commerce than ever, and educating ourselves more than ever? The reality is that new media, while speeding up our access to all parts of the globe, have enhanced our social need for personal contact—what John Naisbitt correctly referred to as "high tech/high touch" in his first *Megatrends* opus. In effect, as our technological ability to communicate has accelerated globally, so too has our need to commune in person, with family, friends, and people whom we will never meet again.

The concept of the "new media revolution" is exploded with surgical precision by Brian Winston in his highly informative 1986 book *Misunderstanding Media*, in which he refers to "... the law of the suppression of radical potential." In this highly detailed revisionist approach to perceiving "inventions" as "revolutionary," Winston posits:

> The "law" of the suppression of radical potential explains the delay of the introduction of television into the United States which lasted at least seven years, excluding the years of war. It explains the period from around 1880 to the eve of the First War, during which the exercise and control of the telephone (in both the U.S. and the U.K.) was worked out while its penetration was much reduced. It accounts for the delays holding up the long playing record for a generation and the videocassette recorder for more than a decade. It underlies the halt in the growth of all but through-air propagation of audiovisual signals for more than twenty years in most countries (p. 25).

Winston goes on to state,

> The "law" works in the broadest possible way to ensure the survival, however battered, of family, home, workplace, church, president and queen, and above

all, it preserves the great corporation as the primary institution of our society (p. 25).

In other words, it may seem as if a revolution is in progress, but in fact the changes are incremental in the short to intermediate term. It is only over the long term that the major shifts can be observed. So the reader may be asking, "If these changes are incremental, how come things seem different to me?" The answer is Rome was not built in a day, the Russian Revolution did not happen in a twinkling, and the demise of the former Soviet Union did not occur because Gorbachev willed it. As the performer Eddie Cantor is alleged to have said, "It took me 25 years to become a hit overnight." The same is true with the influence of technology. The so-called flattening of American organizations is not an overnight sensation. The pressures to flatten have been building for over 150 years. It is just that in the last 10 to 15 years we have begun to tune in to the organizational tremors caused by electronic media.

The good news is that electronic media are not about to fade away. On the contrary, they will continue their inexorable march into every milieu. The appropriate strategy is to engage these media to best advantage (lest, like the gigantic glaciers of the last Ice Age, they crush you while you stand in their path). It is equally advantageous to attempt to understand the evolving roles of managers and employees, and to engage this understanding for future success.

Chapter 3

Electrovisual Media and the American Corporation

In the last ten years or so American corporations have been downsizing. Moreover, they are flattening. Much of this flattening and the concomitant subversion of American corporate middle managers is due in large measure to the advent of the electrovisual media described in the previous chapter—the telephone, videotape, teleconferencing, computers and computer networks, and the Internet and World Wide Web. In effect, these electrovisual media have contributed to the breakdown of hierarchy—the so-called traditional top-down, militaristic/bureaucratic, pyramid structure—in American corporations. What we are witnessing is the transition of the American firm from the militaristic/bureaucratic style typical of the 1950s manufacturing firm to an organizational architecture that is more dynamic and flexible.

The Evolving American Corporation

Robert J. Samuelson in his *The Good Life and its Discontents: The American Dream in the Age of Entitlement 1945–1995* (Times Books, 1995) poses the following question: "... why did Corporate America, which had seemed so successful and stable in the 1950s and 1960s, later become so convulsed?" It is a good question and Samuelson answers "... the larger answer seems to be that many big companies were hit simultaneously by similar forces: harsh recessions, new competitors and the legacies of past overconfidence—poor products and high costs." Samuelson points out that beginning in the 1970s, profit margins (profits as a share of sales) plunged. In the 1950s, they averaged nearly 17 percent; by the 1980s, they were less than 9 percent. Samuelson adds, "The declines triggered waves of cost cutting, including layoffs. If companies hadn't cut costs, they faced market loss, hostile takeovers or even bankruptcy."

While we are not inclined to argue with Samuelson's economic prowess, we must add another perspective. The decline in profit margins seems to coincide with the proliferation of electrovisual media in the American organization, such as the telephone, videocassette, and computer—a proliferation that continues to this day in the form of the personal computer, mobile telephony, and the Internet. What has happened to American corporations in terms of their structure and attendant manager–employee relationships is, we think, a direct result of the conflict between the rapid flow of communication fostered by speed-of-light electronic communications media, on the one hand, and the slowness and ploddingness of the pyramid organizational hierarchy fostered by a paper-based structure.

The paper-based communications structure of the American corporation, with its inherent layers of middle managers, has been competing (and perhaps warring) for several decades now with the informal communications flow among organizational entities created by electronic media. Clearly, the telephone is faster than the mail room; a videocassette of an executive presentation is faster than waiting for the executive to make a field trip; the teleconference is faster than waiting for the middle manager to "explain it all"; e-mail is faster than snail mail.

It is possible that the profit margins of American corporations have declined significantly in the last several decades because electronic media (which have flourished in the same time period and continue to do so) have moved information faster than the structure in which they have been used could cope with it. It is possible that these electronic media, because of their speed and efficiency, exposed the inherent inefficiency of the bureaucratic, pyramid organizational structure that for so long had nurtured corporate America. The fallout from this conflict of communications systems has been evident for some time. For example, since 1987 American corporations, particularly large ones, have been shrinking. The *New York Times*, for instance, reported in a 1992 front page article that ". . . big companies are continuing to cut [jobs]—a trend that promises to keep the pace of [the economic] recovery slow" (December 17, 1992, p. 1). The article goes on to say, "A recent survey of more than 800 companies by the American Management Association found that one in four companies is planning work force reductions by the middle of 1993. That is the highest level since the research group began its survey six years ago." Examples of job-cutting companies included IBM (25,000 jobs) and General Motors (18,000 jobs). In other words, American corporations are getting thinner, not just in terms of numbers of employees but also in terms of layers of management.

Is there a correlation between the saturation of American corporations by electrovisual media, such as the computer, satellites, and videotape, and the apparent evolving general organizational structure of these corporations? Has the advent of electrovisual media changed the nature of the relationship among top management, middle management, and lower level employees? Has the burgeoning use of electrovisual media changed both the formal and informal organizational structure of American corporations in the last 40+ years? The answer to these questions is in the affirmative.

It is our contention that since the late 1950s and continuing to the present day electrovisual media have altered, albeit sometimes blatantly, sometimes subtly, the relationship between American corporate managers and employees: The relationship between American corporate executives and various internal and external publics is becoming far more fluid and dynamic as a direct result of the increasing use of electrovisual media, as opposed to the bureaucratic/militaristic model typical of American corporate organizations. Moreover, American corporate managers, particularly middle managers, are far more vulnerable today than ever because of the shift in communication patterns created as a direct result of the increasing use of electrovisual media. This vulnerability is evidenced by the tens of thousands of corporate employees (particularly middle managers) who have been displaced in the last 10 to 15 years.

Technology Diffusion

Once media became standardized and portable, for example, as with the videocassette in 1971 (Marlow and Secunda, 1991, p. 19) and microcomputers in 1975 (Rogers, 1986, p. 25), corporate managers began to use these media for a growing variety of communication purposes. Clearly, the use of videotape in the nonbroadcast context, for example, has gone far beyond original expectations. In the early stages a handful of individuals and organizations enthusiastically adopted the medium. Today there doesn't seem to be any organization that does not take the VCR for granted, even though it has taken decades for the medium to become truly part of the "corporate communications" landscape. The adoption of videotape in the nonbroadcast (or corporate context) over a period of 40+ years very much parallels the observations of Gabriel Tarde. As Everett M. Rogers reports in *Communication Technology*, "Tarde observed that the rate of adoption of a new idea usually followed an S-shaped curve over time: At first, only a few individuals adopt a new idea, then the rate of adoption spurts as a large number of individuals accept the innovation, and, finally, the adoption slackens as only a few individuals are left to adopt" (pp. 72–73).

With respect to videotape, only a few individuals and organizations adopted the medium in the late 1950s. It wasn't until the early 1970s, when Sony introduced the standardized and highly portable 3/4-inch U-Matic videocassette, that "a large number of individuals" accepted the innovation. And while the so-called nonbroadcast television market has grown from a $207 million industry in the early 1970s to a $6 billion plus market in the 1990s, the rate of growth has slackened in the last five years, suggesting strongly that "only a few individuals are left to adopt."

From its earliest uses (relevant to distribution), videotape was primarily used in centralized or regional areas—the distribution area for a program was constrained. Following the introduction of the 3/4-inch videocassette, the distribution of videotaped messages extended beyond centralized and regional areas to include all company locations, whether domestic or international. With the 1/2-inch videocassette and growth of the home VCR market, companies extended their distribution of videotaped messages into the home. If we liken the technology diffusion history of videotape to a stone dropped into a pool, perhaps we can describe the diffusion of the technology in the early stages as the first ripple in the water, and in the later stages as the larger ripples.

The same kind of analogy can be made in terms of the ascending use of the medium hierarchically before and after 1971, that is, before and after the advent of the 3/4-inch videocassette. Before 1971, top management was conspicuous in its absence from its direct use of the medium. After 1971, this pattern was reversed. The presence of top management in videotaped messages to employees or external audiences seems almost concurrent with the introduction of the 3/4-inch videocassette. Once a cost-efficient distribution medium was available, top management appears to have taken immediate advantage of it.

The adoption of teleconferencing, computing technology, and now the Internet is similar in pattern to that of videotape and Tarde's S-shaped curve. Moreover, the economics of teleconferencing and computing technologies fits the classic pattern: As the number of adopters increased, the unit price decreased, which, in turn, stimulated the adoption of the technology by even larger numbers of users.

The Breakdown of Hierarchy

Top management's use of the videotape medium, particularly after 1971, implies a significant change in management style, organizational structure, and communications. Prior to 1971, with top management reportedly absent from the use of videotape as a communications medium, the typical organizational structure of the times—the hierarchical bureaucracy, based largely on a military/industrial model—was intact. Top managers were invisible. They remained in their boardrooms talking among themselves. They communicated with their subordinates, who, in turn, communicated corporate policies to lower level subordinates, until ultimately "orders" were received by workers at the line level.

Even the term *line* management implies a militaristic model. It is the kind of characteristic media and culture analyst Marshall McLuhan might have dubbed "mechanistic." Economic historian Harold Innis (McLuhan's intellectual precursor) might have interpreted this kind of organizational model as "monopolistic" in terms of the communications flow, that is, communication flows from the top of the organization down until the workers at the bottom line of the so-called organizational chart get the "message." With videotaped messages, especially those in which top management appear, the typical hierarchical organization chart was implicitly subverted. Not only did top management become "visible" (although not in the flesh), they were also communicating directly with line workers, in effect subverting the bureaucratic authority (and communications monopoly) of middle managers.

This is particularly reflected in the use of the medium for employee news. The vast majority of employee news programs are reportedly produced by workers who are not even in middle management, employees not that far from the bottom rung of the organizational chart. In many instances, these employees have chosen the content of employee news programs, providing higher level managers with an upward flow of information about employees and the company's operations that without videotape might have gone uncommunicated.

Overall, the videotape medium, based on the reports of users, seems to have contributed, by implication, to the creation of a communications environment that runs counter to the bureaucratic/militaristic hierarchy typical of the post World War II era. A similar statement could be made about teleconferencing. Ironically, the growing use of so-called business television (the video side of teleconferencing) is a throwback to the old days of live broadcast television. In this instance, a live performance (with perhaps some canned videotaped sequences) is beamed via satellite to one or more locations (perhaps domestic, sometimes international). Some organizations have permanently installed business television facilities. J.C. Penney, for example, was one of the earliest users of business television. It "broadcasts" daily programs from its Dallas headquarters to buyers to inform them of developments in products, prices, and policies. In a very meaningful way, this business television network circumvents J.C. Penney's middle management. Top management goes directly from policy decision-making management to the retail level in an electrovisual instant.

The computer and computer networks provide a similar example. Today, tens of thousands of low-level clerks (defined by *Megatrends* author John Naisbitt as "the" job that defines the labor landscape of the second half of the 20th century) have access to mounds of information that heretofore went unshared. They also have communications access with other "clerks" in a multitude of other organizations. On the other hand, through the use of computers and computer networks, top managers have greater access to up-to-date information, that is, their span of control is wider and dynamic. As a result, the role of middle managers as "carriers" of information to and from top management and lower management and employees has become deflated. The Internet and the World Wide Web exacerbate this evolving communications environment.

In sum, over a 40+ year period the videotape, teleconferencing, and computer media have contributed to the creation of a communications flow that has reordered the multilevel corporate organization to the detriment of middle management's role and authority. The communication environment, therefore, has become susceptible to being more holistic, open, and free flowing, as opposed to the more rigid, closed, manual (print) oriented organization reflected in the bureaucratic/militaristic organizational hierarchy. These observations tend to support Harold Innis' (1951) contention that new technologies have a bias toward either time or space. The videotape, teleconferencing, and computer electrovisual media clearly are space biased—they transcend the physical boundaries of nations and transcend the organizational boundaries of "departments," "management levels," and "programming distributors." Innis' contention that new technologies have the capacity to upend monopolies also finds support in the evidence. By implication, because these media can transcend organizational boundaries, they have the potential for breaking up the "informational" monopoly created by hierarchical conceptions of the corporate culture.

The evidence indicates that the videotape medium, for example, did not remain in the hands of a few television broadcasters or producers, or in the trade show booth, or in the role-playing room, or in corporate conference rooms. To the contrary, the technology reached out beyond fixed (studiobound) situations and gained access to various parts of the American culture through reduced cost of ownership and portability. The medium sought audiences beyond the confines of the physical studio. However, over time, and particularly with the advent of the videocassette format (which liberated the use of the medium for production, editing, and distribution), the medium was used for communicating to an ever-widening audience in physical terms.

The Future Structure of American Corporations

"The typical large organization, such as a large business or a government agency, twenty years hence will have no more than half the levels of management of its counterpart today, and no more than a third the number of 'managers.'" (Drucker, 1989, p. 207). Drucker goes on to say, "In its structure, and in its management problems and concerns, it will bear little resemblance to the typical manufacturing company, circa 1950, which our textbooks still consider the norm . . . the business, and increasingly the government agency as well, will be knowledge-based, composed largely of specialists who direct and discipline their own performance through organized feedback from colleagues and customers. It will be an information-based organization" (p. 207).

Drucker's 1989 comment echoes a "recommendation" made nine years earlier by management consultant John Diebold in a 1980 speech to the Harvard Business School Club in Washington, D.C. In this speech Diebold urged managers, "Take into account the fact that nearly all work will have to become less hierarchically organized, with much less of the boss–subordinate relationship. Most firms will come to realize that this is in their best economic interest." (Diebold, 1982, pp. 49–50). Diebold's vision is a strong "suggestion." In the intervening years reality, created by electronic media, has pressured organizations to yield to the concept of the breakdown of traditional hierarchy.

Drucker, in the more recent *Managing in a Time of Great Change,* surmises:

> When, during the past ten or fifteen years, companies began to organize themselves internally around the flow of information—we now call it "reengineering"—they immediately found that they did not need a good many management levels. Some companies have since cut two-thirds of their management layers. Now that we are beginning to organize around external information, we are learning that the economy needs far fewer intermediaries. We are eliminating wholesalers (p. 169).

In other words, in addition to shifting decision-making authority, organizations will continue to *flatten* structurally. Marlow, in *Managing Corporate Media,* an examination of the evolving use of electrovisual media, such as videotape, teleconferencing, and computers in American corporations, also concluded that organizations will tend to be flatter, that layers of middle management will be eliminated and management span of control will be extended (p. 162).

Authors Marc S. Gerstein and Robert B. Shaw seem to concur with this view. In a chapter entitled "Organizational Architectures for the Twenty-First Century" (*Organizational Architecture*, 1992) they state:

> The 1990s may witness the beginning of the end of the traditional organization. A century dominated by a single type of organization—the machine bureaucracy—is slowly giving way to a new era. Driven by . . . eight forces [including technology] . . . , organizations are being forced to reshape themselves to survive and to prosper (p. 263).

The authors conclude, "Information technology has begun to revolutionize organizational design by providing alternatives to hierarchy as the primary means of coordination. Information systems, common architectures, shared data bases, decision support tools, and expert systems facilitate the coordination of behavior without control through hierarchy, thus enabling the creation of autonomous units linked together through information."

Authors Malone and Rockart also point to the limitations of traditional hierarchies: "Central decision makers can become overloaded and therefore unable to cope effectively with rapidly changing environments or to consider enough information about complex issues. Furthermore, people at the bottom may feel left out of the decision making and as a result be less motivated to contribute their efforts" (p. 133). The authors also surmise that ". . . what appears to be happening is a paradoxical combination of centralization and decentralization. Because information can now be distributed more easily, people lower in the organization can now become well enough informed to make more decisions more effectively. At the same time, upper-level managers can more easily review decisions made at lower levels. Thus, because lower-level decision makers know they are subject to spot-checking, senior managers can retain or even increase their central control over decisions" (p. 133).

Is it a mere coincidence that the mechanistic, militaristic, bureaucratic style of American corporate management and organizational architecture typical of the manufacturing organization is evolving into a more fluid, dynamic "information-based" system at the same time that many of the world's leading nations have apparently come to the conclusion that war (at least on a large, mass scale) does not pay? Or, to put it in even more economic terms, that a military style of management and organizational architecture just does not flow to the bottom line as it once did? Is it a mere coincidence that a generation after the introduction of several major electrovisual technologies (the computer, videotape, and satellites, among them) the shape of American corporations appears to be changing?

It is reminiscent of the 40 years Moses and the emerging Jewish people wandered in the desert allowing the old "slave" mentality generation to die off and the new "free men" generation to enter the "promised land." But as contemporary events are reminding us, the "promised land" of technology is not without its pain.

Where Will All the People Go?

Everett Rogers (1986) points out that "One of the most serious social problems in the Information Society is unemployment" (p. 165). His view—expressed prior to the October 1987 stock market crash, the ensuing real estate crash, and the seemingly never ending announcements of corporate layoffs in the last five years—was not optimistic. He said, ". . . there is no obvious place for former industrial workers to be absorbed. Will Information Societies be able to provide jobs in services and information for the large number of industrial workers who will be unemployed by such information technologies as robots, word-processors, and computers? The answer is: probably not" (p. 165). He further stated, "Industrial manufacturing is the chief target for computer automation, with the office close behind. One of the direct impacts of such computer-based technologies as office automation and robotics is to decrease labor, which is replaced by capital" (p. 166).

Rogers' pessimism appears to be justified in view of the corporate lay-offs described earlier. And it appears clear that information technologies have contributed significantly to the rise in unemployment in the last five years in the United States. Perhaps, though, what we are painfully observing and living through is yet another displacement of workers in another phase of the electronic age that began almost 158 years ago. New technologies and innovations do cause displacements, as Harold Innis and Marshall McLuhan have observed. But to say that these displacements are permanent is to ignore a long history of technological innovation and their effects.

For example, humans as an inherently communicating species have gone through various phases with respect to communications technologies. First came speech. Language probably existed in the Cro-Magnon period circa 35,000 B.C. We also know that prehistoric humans created cave paintings circa at least 22,000 B.C. (Rogers, 1986, p. 25). The Print Era probably began roughly in 4,000 B.C., when the Sumerians wrote on clay tablets (Innis, 1951). Then came the Greeks, who in circa 700 B.C. standardized the phonetic alphabet, which, according to Eric Havelock in *Origins of Western Literacy*, gave rise to Western Civilization as we know it. The print revolution continued with the development of the Gutenberg printing press in 1455, which further standardized the process of printing. And it has been argued that this development gave rise to the Industrial Revolution several centuries later.

The Electronic Age was inaugurated in 1838 when Samuel Morse transmitted the first telegraph message. Since then all manner of electronic, telecommunications, and interactive devices have been invented and diffused into our culture on a seemingly global scale. All through these eras people mired in older technologies have been temporarily displaced by workers using newer technologies, sometimes with violent effects. But ultimately all willing workers became employed in some capacity.

A parallel to this observation is that newer technologies do not necessarily replace older technologies, contrary to McLuhan's contention. Broadly speaking, newer technologies add to the communications technology landscape, that is, they enable us to do something that we couldn't do before. This something is in addition to pre-existing technological capabilities. For example, when print came along, we did not all of a sudden stop using speech. When electronic technologies came along, we did not all of a sudden stop using print.

The history of communications technology is like looking at a cross section of the Grand Canyon. The lower layers represent the earlier communications technologies; the higher levels, the newest. In a meaningful way, the more recent communications technologies are built upon the capabilities of the earlier technologies. And the process continues to this day.

Ultimately displaced workers will be absorbed by other companies. But it is unlikely that new employment will come from large organizations.

Small companies will continue to provide the largest opportunities for employment. For example, Malone and Rockart (1991), discussing the impacts of computer networks conclude, "... We expect networks to lead to less vertical integration—more buying rather than making—and to the proliferation of smaller firms" (pp. 131–132). Some of the displaced workers may ultimately be rehired by the firms that laid them off. A 1991 survey by the Wyatt Company, examining the results of cutbacks at more than 1,000 companies in the previous five years, found that two thirds of the companies simply slashed their payrolls without trying to eliminate the amount of work. And more than 80 percent of the companies were later forced to replace 10 percent or more of the people they let go because necessary work was going undone (*New York Times*, December 17, 1992, p. D20).

Over 25 years ago, T.C. Helvey, in *The Age of Information* wrote, "Man will rely more and more on transmitted and decoded information, and his survival will not depend only on his physical fitness, but on the quality of his communications system." Today those communications systems— videotape, teleconferencing, computer networks—continue to permeate every institution. These same systems have not only added to corporate management's ability to manage, they have also caused a reshaping of the very institutions that have harnessed them, leading to the displacement (and displeasure) of tens of thousands of workers. This process appears to have no end in the short term. Ultimately there will be some period of economic equilibrium, as *Millennium* author Jacques Attali points out. This current period, however long it will last, can be viewed as problematic, or as an opportunity. For those with managerial bent, it can be viewed as an opportunity.

In 1991 authors Malone and Rockart, writing in *Scientific American*, stated, "Clearly, this world will require services, both automated and human, to filter the tremendous amount of information available. In general, as the amount of information increases, people who can creatively analyze, edit, and act on information in ways that cannot be automated will become even more valuable" (p. 136).

Drucker adds, "Information is data endowed with relevance and purpose. Converting data into information thus requires knowledge. And knowledge, by definition, is specialized ... The information-based organization requires far more specialists overall than does the command-and-control structure we are accustomed to" (Drucker, 1989, pp. 209–210). Drucker also pointed to other conclusions that are in part the fallout from the spread of electronic media. Among the points he emphasized are the following:

> Information is replacing authority (p. 3).

> Now that knowledge is taking the place of capital as the driving force in organizations worldwide, it is all too easy to confuse data with knowledge and information technology with information (p. 13).

In postcapitalism, power comes from transmitting information to make it productive, not from hiding it (p. 14).

The new organizations need to go beyond senior–junior polarities to a blend with sponsor and mentor relations (p. 17).

The doomsayers notwithstanding, mass unemployment is not likely. In fact, new technologies, while causing short-term displacements, usually provide opportunities for entrepreneurialship, which, in turn, create jobs. In the future, continue to look to small business for job opportunities. Because of the accelerated flow of information, electrovisual technologies have gradually contributed to the obsolescence of the traditional social contract between employer and employee that provided an employee with opportunities, advancement, and stability in return for company loyalty and hard work. A new world economic order is evolving, and with it numerous problems. But it also a time when more fulfilling and productive work environments can be created.

Chapter 4

The Emerging Corporate Landscape

In the previous chapters we have positioned that electronic media in various linear and interactive forms have significantly altered the structure of American corporations and the relationship between management and employees. In this chapter, we will describe some of the other major forces exacting strong influence on the changing corporate landscape and, in turn, corporate communications. The forces we view as most critical to evaluate are the trends toward downsizing and upsizing, and the new employment contract within the context of this rapidly changing landscape. Davidow and Malone (1992) capture the essence of this change, in this excerpt from their book, *The Virtual Corporation*:

> Without a doubt, the new business revolution will be a shock to the system, a blow to our sensibilities. It will require new social contracts, ever-higher levels of general education, and a frightening degree of trust. . . . For many firms the challenge of all of this change will prove too great. For some employees, the experience will be more traumatic than that of changes demanded by past industrial transformations—though the threat this time won't be regimentation, exploitation, or dehumanization but unpredictability, lack of comfortable structure, and simply, too much responsibility. Executive careers spent building power and influence may turn out to be superfluous. Workers content to put in their hours and go home, may suddenly find themselves saddled with responsibility and control they never desired" (Davidow and Malone, 1992, p. 7).

To understand the impact of these radical changes in the corporate landscape, consider the following:

- Small businesses account for 70 percent of the economy in 1993. Companies employing fewer than 100 workers accounted for over 90 percent of all job growth since 1988.
- People who are computer literate make an average of 10 to 15 percent more than their counterparts who do not.
- The average American worker will most likely work in ten or more different types of jobs and at least five different companies before he or she retires.
- Firms with fewer than 20 employees added 4.4 million new jobs between 1987 and 1991, with slightly larger firms adding another 1.4 million.
- America dominates the worldwide computer software market, estimated at $72 billion.
- The United States has a massive lead in financial services, both in productivity and know-how.
- Jobs as we've known them will cease to exist. Rather, people will come together for a particular project and disband when the work is complete. Temporary teams will abound.
- Electronic networks will make the world a single market, where experts and specialists can be found and moved or telecommute to the project.
- By the year 2000, classic factory workers will be less than 16 percent of the total U.S. population.
- Management is on the decline, moving from 33 to 22 percent and falling.
- Nearly 45 million people, more than one third of the American workforce, are either self-employed or working as temps, part-timers, or consultants. This contingent workforce has grown 57 percent since 1980.
- Knowledge workers (professionals and technical workers) are the fastest growing segment of the workforce, predicted to be 20 percent by 2005.
- Marketable managers are specialists with generalists tendencies, adding definite value to the work of the organization.
- Companies that contract noncore processes to outside resources have revenues 22 percent higher than counterparts who do not do so.
- Forty-one million Americans work at home, which is 33 percent of the total workforce.
- Office work rather than office workers will do the traveling—telecommuting is on the increase.
- The paternalistic model of cradle-to-grave employment is dead and buried.
- *Executive Recruiter News* estimates that at least 125,000 professionals labor as temps every day. Their share of the $25 billion annual temporary work market has doubled, to about $1.3 billion in 1992.

Source: *Career Systems Advantage, Inc.* "The Changing Landscape of Work" (unpublished white paper).

We now turn to an examination of the two major forces that have augured the just-described transformations, upsizing and downsizing, and the emerging employment contract.

Upsizing, Downsizing, and Corporate Responsibility

The prevalence of corporate restructuring, whether by choice or by default, amidst continually changing environments is underscored in the following passage from *The Virtual Corporation*: ". . . companies content to maintain status quo indefinitely may not only encounter change but be forced to endure continuous, unremitting, almost unendurable transmutation" (Davidow and Malone, 1992, p. 7). This sets the tone for the following section, which explores the forces of upsizing and downsizing and the corporation's responsibility for the effects thereof.

Upsizing: Competition Through Acquisition

In 1995, many companies experienced the transmutation described by Davidow and Malone, which saw an unprecedented $458 billion in mergers and acquisition deals by U.S. companies. This record was up 32 percent from the previous record of $347 billion reached in 1994. As companies feel the pressure to join forces to stay competitive and to manage the rapid change in information and technology, major mergers took place and transformed entire industries, and thus the corporate landscape, in the process. Some of the more significant mergers and acquisitions that took place in 1995 were as follows (*Wall Street Journal*, January 2, 1996, p. R8):

- Walt Disney Company purchased Capital Cities/ABC for $18.5 billion.
- Chemical Bank Corp. agreed to a $10 billion merger pact with Chase Manhattan Corp.
- First Interstate Bancorp was purchased in a hostile takeover by Wells Fargo Co. for $11.6 billion.
- Hoechst AG bought Marion Merrell Dow Inc. for $7.1 billion.
- Kimberly-Clark Corp. bought rival Scott Paper Company, for $7.4 billion.
- Seagram Co. bought 80 percent of MCA for $5.7 billion.
- Westinghouse Electric bought CBS Inc. for $5 billion.

Evidence abounds that employers are facing growing pressures to follow growth-oriented strategies. Many businesses are just now learning the ropes about global competition for customers as an adjunct to, or even replacement for, long-acknowledged competition about technology. As a result of this growing pressure, companies are opting to "buy" rather than "make" the requisite expertise, technologies, and customers it requires to remain competitive.

One of the greatest challenges that results from amassing these behemoth structures is, of course, communication. As previously separate cultures, technologies, and expertise are brought together under one parent company, communication clashes occur as complexity rises. Certainly, incompatible cultures and technological systems are forces to be reckoned with once an acquisition has occurred. But the greatest communication challenge is that of knowledge or expertise management, as company's with a wealth of expertise or "intellectual capital" tend to be the most likely targets for acquisition by a larger, perhaps less expert, parent company.

Some organizations have begun to take on this complex challenge of expertise management. In terms of intellectual capital, Jensen (1995) sees a "knowledge troika" of simplicity, clarity, and integration that will guide future organizations who have invested heavily in this asset. We suggest that this troika will also help guide organizations through the maze of communication challenges inherent in acquisitions as well. According to a 1994 study of knowledge management's impact on corporate success, conducted by Jensen Communications Group, 80 percent of the respondents that created simplify/clarify/integrate changes were top quartile performers. The study shows that the normal strategies for affecting change in employee behavior are less critical than the commitment to integrate all the strategies. This underscores an important theme found throughout this book: Because communication amidst change is complex, organizations need to recognize the variety of forces impacting them and integrate several strategies that respond to the myriad communication challenges.

Downsizing: Growth Through Reduction

The most frequent and most socially disruptive restructuring action in the 1980s and 1990s was downsizing. The dominant reasons given for restructuring are competitive pressure and economic recession. As such, the communicated goals of most organizations were primarily financial in nature, assuming that a direct relationship between a decline in the staff numbers and financial growth exists. In reality, most organizations fell far from achieving these goals, as can be seen from the results of a 1993 study by Wyatt on the restructuring practice of 531 U.S. companies (Table 4.1).

The most striking result, although not surprising, was that which related to the "increase competitive advantage" goal. It is a widely held belief that the organizations need to be "lean and mean" in order to remain competitive. We would not disagree that this is an intelligent benchmark to strive for, but we would argue that organizations ran head-long into downsizing campaigns without understanding the full ramifications of their actions in the long term.

Table 4.1   Restructuring goal achievement figures (top five). SOURCE: Parkington, John. Best Practices in Corporate Restructuring; Wyatt's 1993 Survey of Corporate Restructuring.

Goal	Percent who said it was a goal	Percent who achieved goal
Reduce Expenses	89%	46%
Increase Profitability	83%	32%
Increase ROI	60%	21%
Increase Productivity	71%	22%
Increase Competitive Advantage	67%	19%

Competitiveness was not enhanced because organizations, in part, in becoming "lean" cut or lost some of their greatest competitive "muscle" in terms of intellectual assets. Furthermore, organizations ignored, and continue to ignore, the devastating effects that downsizing has on the corporate culture and the society within which the organization is attempting to thrive. As competitiveness is an organizational attribute intrinsically linked to the relative psychological health of the employees charged with sustaining it, downsized firms exchanged long-term competitiveness for short-term financial gains.

In addition to the fact that most of the companies surveyed failed to reach their financial goals, tens of thousands of employees lost both their jobs and their trust in corporate America. To lend insight into the magnitude of job loss resulting from downsizing, by New Years Eve, 1995, it is estimated that the number of people laid off from their jobs since the beginning of 1989 reached three million. The November 1995 cutbacks of 41,293 jobs were up 45 percent from levels the year earlier. Furthermore, published "jobless count" statistics only tells part of the story in that they are computed by looking at the numbers of individuals on unemployment assistance. Those individuals who chose not to take unemployment assistance or whose assistance has run out and are still unemployed are not counted, which is a dramatic portion. Further, "joblessness" only applies to the individual who lost the job, not the millions who are affected, such as spouses, children, and elders who relied on this income and security to survive and thrive.

As if the fact that the continual practice of ineffective downsizing tactics in troubled companies isn't enough of a blow to the workforce, an increasing number of healthy companies are looking at this radical surgery as a way to bolster stock prices. AT&T, which is profitable and growing, announced in 1996 that it would cut 40,000 jobs, or 13 percent of its staff, as part of its previously announced reorganization into three separate companies. In New Jersey, where AT&T is the largest employer, it will shed 7,000 jobs (*New York Times*, January 7, 1996, p. B2). At the end of first quarter of 1995, Mobil Corp. posted soaring first-quarter earnings of $636 million, a turnaround from their 1994 loss of $145 million. One week later it announced plans to eliminate 4,700 jobs. The combination of these two announcements resulted in the stock price of Mobil rising to a 52-week high.

The impact of such purely profit-motivated moves on the collective psyche of the workforce is devastating. No longer can companies hide behind poor performance as the reason for downsizing measures; it has become painfully clear to the American workforce that downsizing is a weapon that will be wielded whenever an organization wants to improve its numbers, or more correctly, to lend the appearance of doing so to its shareholders. While some organizations espouse an alliance to and recognition of all of its "stakeholders," including customers, employees, and shareholders, it would seem that shareholders are driving the decisions in most American corporations, although other disconfirming information clouds the picture.

For example, 1995 was a very good year for earnings, yet corporations paid out a record low proportion of their profits to shareholders. Employees did no better; compensation rose by only 2.7 percent, the lowest increase in fourteen years. If financial soundness is the driving force behind downsizing efforts, where do all these accrued profits go? Certainly, CEO and other executive salaries are reaching record highs; this could account for some of the profits. It is also theorized that by holding on to more of their earnings, companies are able to expand, invest, and save for a "rainy day"—a bit of a paradox considering the number of downsizing efforts in place and the resultant record numbers of unemployed workers. If the prevailing corporate environment does not qualify for a "rainy day," what exactly are these companies waiting for?

The effects of downsizing on corporate communication can be devastating as well. Fear and uncertainty tend to close down communication channels at the exact time when expansive communication is the most effective response. This tendency is in direct opposition to what organizations should strive for when the aftereffects of downsizing are settling in, as we have learned from studies on survivors that their greatest need during times of uncertainty is for information. Communication amidst a downsizing is also greatly hampered by "reversals" made by management. For example, a company may tell its employees that the downsizing is a one-time event and then find itself in the position of having to communicate the likelihood of yet another. The obvious impact on the corporate culture is a dramatic decrease in trust—just the opposite of what we feel is required to effectively communicate amidst constant change.

Corporate Failure and Social Responsibility

Certainly, the failure of many American corporations to adapt to changing economic circumstances has evolved from being solely a collection of business drawbacks to a major social concern. The adverse impacts of failure have become familiar to us all: increased workloads, lowered morale, lowered commitment to the employer, decreased willingness to take risks, decreased productivity, decreased job satisfaction, and inability on the part of the companies to attract and retain high-performing employees.

Many reasons have been offered for these failures, from rigid corporate cultures and cumbersome hierarchies, such as that of Mercedes-Benz (Miller and Aeppel, 1993) to the inability of top management to grasp early on the importance of the Japanese competition, as was the case with General Motors. Levinson (1994) views these as the ostensible reasons, but they do not explain adequately the roots of corporate failure. He views the explanations as fundamentally psychological, having to do with such dynamics as individual and organizational narcissism, unconscious recapitulation of family dynamics in the organization, exacerbating dependency, and psychologically illogical organizational structure and compensation schemes. In order to deal more effectively with such problems, Levinson calls for greater psychological sophistication among boards of directors and senior executives.

What is most interesting is Levinson's inclusion of "inadequate management of change" and "inability to recognize and manage cognitive complexity" within his list of organizational psychological deficiencies. Most organizations certainly view these issues as challenges to be grappled with on a daily basis, but it is doubtful they are recognized for what they are—complex, highly personal challenges that are fraught with the likelihood of failure. This lack of recognition is apparent in corporate communications that attempt to rally the troops around a change initiate, as if sworn consensus makes change any easier to cope with or understand.

Clearly, the inability of organizations to recognize or solve such problems will continue to adversely impact the societal landscape, but it is not nearly that linear a relationship. It is society that is supporting this corporate behavior by owning stock, purchasing products, allowing government to support failing industries, and taking employment with these organizations. The first step in reversing record numbers of failures is to recognize the full weight of the impact the failure has on society, beyond lost jobs, lost self-esteem, decreased loyalty, or battered work ethic. Each of these taken by themselves is destructive enough; taken collectively, the results could be devastating to our very way of life. Organizations, in this way, do hold a tremendous amount of social responsibility, as they are societies in and of themselves in which individuals must learn to live and grow. Corporations that recognize that there are a variety of stakeholders must consider all of the groups when making decisions, employees, shareholders, and customers alike. The new players in the changing landscape hold responsibility for the impact of these changes. As corporations are comprised of employees, it is ultimately the employees who must help effect change that will reverse some of the devastating effects that downsizing has wrought.

The New Employment Contract

As has been discussed, the relationship between employers and employees has changed dramatically and will continue to change in the decades ahead. With loyalty, security, and trust at record lows, a new contract between employers and employees is emerging that will be much more explicit than the implied psychological contract, which has all but vanished from most employees' memories. Requisite worker behaviors in the new landscape will necessarily change, as will individual's disposition toward their careers. In his work *Career Development: Theory & Practice* (1992), Michael Arthur explores these new dimensions, using Weick and Berlinger's (1989) career improvisation factors as a basis: cultivating spiral career concepts, decoupling identity from jobs, preserving discretion, identifying distinctive competence, and synthesizing complex information. Table 4.2 outlines some of Arthur's concepts that have implications for the emerging employment contract.

While much discussion has taken place around the topic of the new employment contract, little attention has been given to the increasing number of violations of the supposedly "advanced" contractual relationships. In a study of violations to the implied psychological contracts that existed between employee and employer, Robinson and Rousseau (1994), found ten types of violations that employers are increasingly committing. Table 4.3 outlines the specific violation types and examples of each as played out in the organizational setting.

The changes in the contract will challenge both employer and employee alike, in some ways evening the playing field between those who hire and those who look to be hired. To this end, growing numbers of workers will work "with" an organization for some specified period of time, in contrast to working "for" a company for some unknown period of time. This workforce has been referred to by a variety of names, such as contingent or temporary, but all epitomize the new employer–employee relationship. As Peter Drucker asserts, "Accept the fact that knowledge workers are volunteers. The 19th-century idea was that the worker needs a job more than we need him. The 20th-century idea is that the worker needs *access* to an organization" (Drucker, 1994). Certainly, effective communication channels will be increasingly relied upon to provide that access.

As organizations continue to change their structures and processes in response to new competitive benchmarks, so too will change the roles taken on by their employees. The new corporate landscape will require a variety of workers, some core, who remain with the organization on a full-time basis; some contingent, who work on a project basis with the organization; and some partners, who work from within the structure of a strategic alliance on an as-needed basis.

Organizations of the future will come to increasingly rely on continually expanding and contracting project teams of contingent workers that will

Table 4.2   Emerging employment contract issues. SOURCE: Arthur, M. B. Career theory in a dynamic context. In D. H. Montross, C. J. Shinkman, eds. *Career Development: Theory & Practice.* Springfield, IL: Charles C. Thomas, 1992, pp. 65–84.

Behavior	Key characteristics and/or behaviors	Prospects for accomodating future workforce
Cultivating Spiral Career Concepts	• Complex career plan that changes often • Incorporates multiple visions of self • Is response to work and nonwork stimulants • Uses trial & error as important sources of information • Makes deliberate & substantial career movements every five to seven years	• Serves to offset expectations about traditional "linear" careers • Allows careers to be acted out in "chunks" so necessary to effective accommodation of work & family • Promises less debilitating effects from parental leave (missing a step on a career ladder is less significant the less ladder-like the career paths) • In contrast to the masculine career arrow, offers greater potential for accommodating feminine perspectives about careers
Decoupling Identity from Jobs	• Relying on job identity begets people who are reluctant to change jobs because of new questions of who they are • Jobs viewed as temporary are less likely to become benchmarks of identity • Emphasizing professional identity that transcends particular job or rank, and "playing" with new career identities allows for thriving in firm self-designing	• Leads to people being less protective about the way jobs are assigned • By keeping, specifics of job at safe psychological distance, thoughts about work, sharing, work redesign, and reallocation of work for increased productivity and better use of workforce become more acceptable • Supervisors' need for control may be more open to change
Preserving Discretion	• Precondition for continuous learning • Can be impeded by a lack of perceived job alternatives by high-commitment situations that screen out fresh ideas • Maintains career insight, continually recognizes	• Preventive or antidote to identification with job, thus reinforcing possibilities of decoupling • Serves to provide a more open marketplace for talent and ideas based on near-term benefits to both individuals and organizations

Continued

Table 4.2   *(Continued)*

Behavior	Key characteristics and/or behaviors	Prospects for accomodating future workforce
	new choices, contributes to self-designing nature of cluster companies (e.g., Silicon Valley) since they feel less obliged to accept any one company's ideas & become more willing to take risks	• Serves to open up new or returning workforce members to compete for vacated positions
Identifying Distinctive Competence	• Assertiveness in promoting one's distinctive competencies, and trust in intuition to transform fragmented information into richer meanings are critical qualities if effective interaction among individuals within self-designing firms is to be achieved • Does not discount importance of bringing diverse skills, competencies, and qualities together toward common goal of continual redesigning of firm	• Suggests more dynamic view of organizations • Decreases dependency on specifics of job or roles and less assumptive about sex-, age-, and race-linked biases • Opens up prospect of recruiting supplementary competence by use of specialists or part-time workers • Makes prospect of working at home more attractive, as people become more valued for the contributions they make, rather than the time they spend at the office
Synthesizing Complex Information	• Facilitates move from idea generation to effective synthesis and implementation of proposals • Ability to integrate patterns of awareness in organizations to larger visions • Ability to articulate how individual contributions fit together • Individuals with this competency will become more valuable to and exercise more influence in the organizations they serve	• Leads to new interpretations of how to use the available workforce • Leads to nurturing of on-the-job learning in a way that benefits both individual and organizational purposes • Reinterprets established models of education, vocational training, and work according to present-day realities

Table 4.3   Types of violations to the psychological contract. SOURCE: Robinson, S.L. and Rousseau, D.M. Violating the psychological contract: Not the exception, but the norm. *Journal of Organizational Behavior* 15(3): 256, 1994.

Violation Type	Definition	Examples
Training/Development	Absence of training or training experience not as promised	"Sales training was promised as an integral part of marketing training. It never materialized."
Compensation	Discrepancies between promised and realized pay, benefits, bonuses	"Specific compensation benefits were promised and were either not given to me or I had to fight for them."
Promotion	Promotion or advancement schedule not as promised	"I perceived a promise that I had a good chance of promotion to manager in one year. While I received excellent performance ratings, I was not promoted in my first year."
Nature of Job	Employer perceived as having misrepresented the nature of the department or the job	"My employer promised I would be working on venture capital projects. I was mainly writing speeches for the CEO."
Job Security	Promises regarding degree of job security one could expect were not met	"The company promised that no one would be fired out of the training angel and that all of us were 'safe' until placement (in return for this security we accepted lower pay). The company subsequently fired four people from the training program."
Feedback	Feedback and reviews inadequate compared with what was promised	"I did not receive performance reviews as promised."
Management of Change	Employees not asked for input or given notice of changes as they were promised	"I was promised more knowledge and control over my future."
Responsibility	Employees given less responsibility and/or	"I was promised greater responsibility, more

Continued

Table 4.3   *(Continued)*

Violation Type	Definition	Examples
	challenge than promised	strategic thinking, and decision making."
People	Employer perceived as having misrepresented the type of people at the firm in terms of things, such as their expertise, work style, or reputation	"I was promised a dynamic and changing environment . . . rubbing elbows with some of the brightest people in the business . . . a big lie. The true picture started to come out . . . after the initial hype . . . of working at one of the best 100 companies in the U.S. had worn off."
Other	Perceived promises not fulfilled by the employer not fit into above categories	"Original representations of the company's financial and market strength that become clearly fraudulent."

come together for a specified purpose and disband once the project is complete. A recent survey of 1,803 U.S. organizations by *Lakewood Publications and Training* magazine (Lakewood Research, 1995) revealed that organizations are increasing their use of the contingent workforce, with 27 percent of public administration firms, 25 percent of business services firms, and 23 percent of manufacturing firms surveyed leading this shift (Lakewood Research, 1995).

Replacing yesterday's criterion of security in return for loyalty, workers in the new landscape will look for opportunities to engage in meaningful work and organizations will continually screen the environment for the best candidate for that work. This phenomenon is underscored by Kanter in *The New Managerial Work*: "Commitment to the organization still matters, but today managers build commitment by offering project opportunities. The new loyalty is not to the boss or to the company, but to projects that actualize a mission and offer challenge, growth, and credit for results"(Kanter, 1989, pp. 88, 91–92).

Kanter goes on to suggest that organizations must find news ways to attract, motivate, and retain talented workers, as this increasingly contingent workforce will continue to scan the landscape for their next project and will feel no loyalty to keep working with a company who provides no implicit rewards, such as challenge and professional development. According to Kanter, organization's embracing the new contract will provide workers with five sources of motivation. We view these sources as the contractual responsibilities of the organization of the future (Kanter, 1989, pp. 88, 91–92):

1. *Mission,* which inspires people to believe in the importance of their work.
2. *Agenda control,* which gives people the opportunity to be in control of their own careers.
3. *Share of value,* which rewards employees for their contribution to the success of the company, based upon measurable results. This can mean that skilled employees earn larger salaries than their putative superiors.
4. *Learning,* which provides people with the chance to learn new skills and develop themselves.
5. *Reputation,* which gives workers a chance to make a name for themselves in terms of public or professional recognition.

As the contract will be more explicit, this is not to say that relationships will not play a key role in the emerging corporate landscape. Employers will need to foster working relationships with the best talent in the workforce and workers will need to develop relationships throughout attractive organizations in order to be considered for the opportunities available for meaningful work. In fact, as the workforce grows more contingent and "virtual," relationships will provide the networks through which work will be found and accomplished. While that is true to some extent in organizations currently, the assumptions that employees understand the cultural nuances and strategic imperatives of the organization cannot be carried over to a contingent population.

The communication challenges inherent in the new contract are formidable. Core employees (including managers and executives) will need to place greater emphasis on communicating *clearly* and *often* with the growing contingent workforce. Further, as mutually agreed-upon contracts are reached, both organizations and workers will need to enhance their communication expertise in the areas of negotiation and contracting. The emerging contracts will be increasingly explicit, committed to in writing, and will contain such essential elements as a compensation agreement, a development agreement, assignment duration, termination provisions, and renewal options (Noer, 1993, pp. 182–184).

Finally, as ambiguity and complexity will reign in the new landscape, with concepts such as "meaningful work" and "feelings of accomplishment" taking on evolving meaning, the ability to manage cognitive complexity will become a crucial competency. Given the boundaryless nature of the new model of work, tolerance for ambiguity will be a key attitudinal shift required of all workers. The temporary nature of contingency work results in great uncertainty of where one will be performing the next project. The rapid changes in organizations and their structures will not allow for reliance on published paradigms or pat prescriptions for career success. Ambiguity will reign, and those who can learn to manage it will be the most successful.

Chapter 5

The New Diversity Benchmark

Recent international developments—passage of the North American Free Trade Agreement (NAFTA) and the formation of the European Union—have led to dramatically increased overseas business opportunities as well as heightened competition for more U.S. companies. As a result, domestic companies now have competition where none existed before and have witnessed niche firms in their industries grow to be formidable players.

As a result of these and other developments, interfacing with other cultures, whether face to face or electronically, has led to the development of global companies. Beyond simply transplanting parts of domestic operations into various foreign countries, the global company not only crosses geographic borders but crosses cultural barriers in its hiring, partnering, strategy development, and most importantly, its communication practices. Global companies set out to strike a synergistic balance between those cultural nuances of the parent company and those of the foreign countries in which they now conduct business, and thus must thrive. By this definition few organizations have truly reached *global* status, although the term is used quite frequently by leading firms who may or may not be close to crossing this threshold.

With the ever-increasing adoption of standardized business practices and communication vehicles, some theorists have predicted the existence of a "seamless business culture" someday that will transcend the culture of its members. Further, it has also been posited that a universal language of business may some day evolve, thus reducing the cultural barriers that now exist. We feel that societies are far from realizing this seamlessness and, as such, must look to enhancing their communication sophistication as it relates to diversity.

Diversity has a deep-rooted impact on communication practices and, in turn, communication effectiveness. Even if common channels and languages are developed, communication will continue to play itself out in the more complex context of diversity, which will in turn impact its effectiveness. In other words, while we may all someday enjoy a common electronic platform, such as that provided by the World Wide Web, the communication practices we employ will still vary dramatically, resulting in less than perfect communication.

In this light, population is the single most important factor governing the size and composition of the labor force, which includes people who are working and those who are looking for work. The U.S. civilian labor force, 127 million in 1992, is expected to reach 151 million by 2005. This projected 19 percent increase represents a slight slowdown in the rate of labor force growth, largely due to slower population growth. As discussed in the following sections, America's workers will be an increasingly diverse group as we move toward 2005. We will examine five types of diversity that are emerging in the new corporate landscape and that hold implications for an organization's ability to communicate effectively: gender diversity, racial diversity, age diversity, cultural diversity, and the most elusive, cognitive diversity.

Gender Diversity

Women will continue to join the labor force in growing numbers. The percentage increase of women in the labor force between 1992 and 2005 will be larger than the percentage increase in the total labor force but smaller than the percentage increase for women in the previous 13-year period. In the late 1980s, the labor force participation of women under age 40 began to increase more slowly than in the past. Women were only 42 percent of the labor force in 1979; by 2005, they are expected to exceed 60 percent.

The Glass Ceiling Commission, set up by the federal government in 1991 to examine the corporate phenomenon of women encountering barriers to entry for the highest level positions, reported last year that while the workforce was 57 percent female, women held just 5 percent of senior management jobs. In books such as *Talking From 9 to 5* by Deborah Tannen and *A Women's Guide to the Language of Success: Communicating With Confidence and Power* by Phyllis Mindell, the gender-based differences of communication have been highlighted and examined as critical sources of communication barriers in the workplace that can lead to fewer high-level promotions for women as compared with men.

Mindell's treatise goes as far to say that until women master the workplace dialect, including indirect orders that are a prerogative of power, they can consider the glass ceiling, a "wall of words." This communication discrimination is occurring despite a variety of emerging theories, one of which is elucidated by Judy B. Rosener in her recent book *America's Competitive Secret*, stating that female executives bring a superior, consensus-building management style to work. For example, Rosener's theories are based, in part, on studies that have concluded that women, while growing up, tended to learn conversation rituals that focus on the rapport dimension of relationships, whereas men tended to learn rituals that focus on the status dimension. These tendencies, which follow us into adulthood, result in men and women who tend to have different habitual ways of saying what they mean, and conversations between them can become the equivalent to crosscultural communications.

As organizations continue to flatten and hierarchies based on status break down through the use of electronic communication, we see opportunities for women to gain a leg up on this wall of words. Eventually women may very well emerge as the more effective gender, with regard to organizational communication. Their tendency to focus on rapport is a critical prerequisite to communicating effectively in the emerging virtual corporate landscape. This may, in turn, help organizations better understand the business implications of valuing gender diversity.

Racial Diversity

Minorities and immigrants will constitute a larger share of the U.S. population in 2005 than they do today. Substantial increases in the number of Hispanics, Asians, and blacks are anticipated, reflecting immigration, and higher birth rates among blacks and Hispanics. Substantial inflows of immigrants will continue to have significant implications for the labor force. Immigrants tend to be of working age but of different educational and occupational backgrounds than the U.S. population as a whole.

White non-Hispanic men will make up a slightly smaller proportion of the labor force, and women and minority group members will comprise a larger share than in 1992. White non-Hispanics have historically been the largest component of the labor force, but their share has been dropping and is expected to fall from 78 percent in 1992 to 73 percent by 2005. The white population is projected to grow more slowly than those of blacks, Asians, and others, but because of their size whites will experience the largest numerical increase. Hispanics will add about 6.5 million workers to the labor force from 1992 to 2005, increasing by 64 percent. Despite this dramatic growth, Hispanics' share of the labor force will only increase from 8 to 11 percent. Blacks, Hispanics, and Asians and other racial groups will account for roughly 35 percent of all labor force entrants between 1992 and 2005.

Little research has been conducted on the communication practices of various racial groups. Racial communication behaviors are often subsumed by cultural nuances, resulting in a greater availability of cultural diversity studies. As such, it is difficult to draw conclusions on the impact that increasing ethnic diversity will impart on corporate communication land-scapes. What can be surmised is that with increasing racial diversity in the workforce, organizations will need to eradicate any racial biases that may continue to exist within their hiring and promoting practices because, if for no other reason, they will not be able to compete without tapping into the communication expertise that resides within an increasingly racially diverse workforce.

Age Diversity

The changing age structure of the population will also directly affect tomor-row's labor force and, in turn, the corporate landscape. Compared with young workers, the pool of experienced workers will increase. In 1992, the median age of the labor force was 37.2 years; by 2005, it will be 40.5 years. Between 1979 and 1992, the youth labor force (16 to 24 years of age) dropped by 5 million, a 20 percent decline. In contrast, the number of youths in the labor force will increase by 3.7 million over the 1992 to 2005 period, reflect-ing an increase of 18 percent, compared with 19 percent growth for the total labor force. As a result, young people are expected to comprise roughly the same percentage of the labor force in 2005 as in 1992. Among youths, the teenage labor force (16 to 19 years of age) will increase by 31 percent over the 1992 to 2005 period, a numerical increase of 2.1 million. The labor force 20 to 24 years of age is projected to increase by 12 percent, a numerical increase of 1.6 million. The total youth labor force accounted for 24 percent of the entire labor force in 1979, fell to 16 percent in 1992, and should stay about the same through 2005.

The scenario should be somewhat different for prime-age workers (25 to 54 years of age). The baby-boom generation will continue to add mem-bers to the labor force, but their share of the labor force peaked in 1985. These workers accounted for 62 percent of the labor force in 1979, and rose significantly to 72 percent in 1992, but should decline slightly to 70 percent by 2005. The proportion of workers in the 25 to 34 age range will decline dramatically, from 28 percent in 1992 to 21 percent in 2005. On the other hand, the growing proportion of workers between the ages of 45 and 54 is equally striking. These workers should account for 24 percent of the labor force by the year 2005, up from 18 percent in 1992. Because workers in their mid-forties to mid-fifties usually have substantial work experience and tend to be more stable than younger workers, this could result in improved pro-ductivity and a larger pool of experienced applicants from which employers may choose.

The number of older workers, aged 55 and above, is projected to grow about twice as fast as the total labor force between 1992 and 2005, and about 15 times as fast as the number of workers aged 55 and above grew between 1979 and 1992. As the baby boomers grow older, the number of workers aged

55 to 64 will increase; they exhibit higher labor force participation than their older counterparts. By 2005, workers aged 55 and over will comprise 14 percent of the labor force, up from 12 percent in 1992.

So what does an aging workforce mean for corporate communications? By sheer tenure, this workforce holds a wealth of experience, which can lend to an organization's ability to harness the power of communication, especially in the area of creating understanding. A more experienced workforce will be able to better understand the complex challenges of communicating in the emerging landscape and can impart their knowledge on those who are less experienced. Conversely, the younger population brings with it less experience but helps bolster an increasing comfort level, if not passion, for change and technological innovation. This is not to say that older workers cannot embrace rapid change and younger workers lack the ability to be sensitive to complexity, but each generation brings both strengths and deficits to the communication culture. Attention to these differences will be critical for organizations as they work to enhance the strengths and to limit the deficits of a multigenerational workforce who must learn to effectively communicate with each other.

Downsizing practices focused on cost reduction have, to a large extent, been biased towards older workers due to the higher salaries they tend to command. By reducing the numbers of more experienced workers through these practices, corporations have decreased their pool of "experience expertise," which is more highly correlated with communication efficacy than functional expertise. Thus, in order to leverage the critical contributions of the older workforce, organizations must revisit those decisions that are biased against the older, more experienced worker.

Cultural Diversity

Cultural diversity within the workforce will continue to increase in dramatic proportions as companies continue to grow their operations overseas and foreign firms continue their influx into the U.S. market. Economists have estimated that 75 percent of the projected growth in international business will come from emerging markets, particularly from China and its "baby dragon" neighbors. This fact alone will force businesses to deal with the cultural differences, most significantly those between East and West, on a magnified scale in the future.

The concept of change epitomizes an interesting example of how the East and West are culturally distinct. While western traditions tend to revere constant, unchanging standards, eastern traditions accept that changing circumstances can justify changes in behavior. For example, to westerners, once contracts are signed these documents are relied upon to enforce dependable, unchanging behavior over time. By contrast, the eastern contract is better defined not as an absolute declaration of the deal but rather as a statement of principles by which signers agree to work together as trustworthy partners (Foster, 1995).

Communication efficacy thus becomes paramount in East–West partnering, as the cultural bases of change orientation are diametrically opposed. Foster (1995) proposes that these opposing forces could complement each other in a business arrangement if the East and West saw themselves as one half of the united, perfect whole they compose together, like the Taoist symbol of yin (stability) and yang (change). While this balanced approach to diversity is an interesting one, it still requires members on both sides of the business team to act as constant translators in order for each side to understand the power and the need of diverse viewpoints. Further, one's orientation to opposing forces, whether they are characterized as contrasting or complementary, strongly influences the ability of a culturally diverse team to work together effectively. In the context of an organization's orientation to change, finding a *balance* between making the change happen and running the risk of adversely impacting something essential to the organism seems to be the key challenge in the survival game (Lee, 1993). While U.S. firms have recognized the opportunities for enhancing change management savvy through the development of culturally diverse workforces, few, if any, are realizing the opportunities that this phenomenon presents for enhancing communication sophistication.

Another challenge presented by cultural diversity is time orientation, that is, its relative abundance or scarcity. This orientation is intricately linked to one's orientation to change and thus holds implications for environments experiencing tumultuous change, such as that being experienced in the United States. As the current ideology around change is that it is characterized as being rapid and constant, our orientation to the relative scarcity of time becomes an important factor that impacts our approach to the challenge of pervasive change. For example, Americans tend to view time as scarce, thus levying pressure to come to completion on projects as quickly as possible. This "results-oriented" attitude is highly valued and rewarded in our culture because it is believed to reflect high competence and a no-nonsense approach to business. But perhaps what it truly reflects is simply a high need for completion and a bias for action due to our orientation towards time. Other cultures, on the other hand, view time as more plentiful, thus exacting an influence on their approach to change management and communication. It is clear that such opposing forces within a culturally diverse workforce can present significant communication challenges to those organizations that wish to be effective in this world of contrasts and complements.

American's inability or unwillingness to adjust to cultural differences is typified in a speech given in Japan by former Secretary of Commerce Baldridge in the Reagan Administration: "If Japan is going to trade (appropriately) with the U.S., it will have to change its culture." (Behrman, 1995). This statement underscores two examples of cultural diversity ignorance: (1) extreme ethnocentricity (our culture is superior to your culture, thus you

should become like us) and (2) the relative malleability of cultural orientation (if your culture is not working for you, you can simply change it). Of
course, neither of these assumptions is true and both can create barriers to
effectively communicating in a culturally diverse landscape. While this may
seem an extreme example, related mindsets are infused into organizations
throughout both the United States and other parts of the world, as we pay lip
service to the importance of being global but, in essence, don't truly understand the sophistication it requires.

This fact is reflected in a study of 1,500 senior executives (of 12 nation-
alities) that explored the extent to which respondents' recognition and
strong convictions around the "increasingly global competitive environment" corresponded to their prioritized dimensions for competing globally
(Reday and Gouillart, 1994). In other words, are corporate leaders willing or
able to "walk the cultural diversity talk?" The researchers delineated such
dimensions as having a global mindset, managing a culturally diverse
workforce, alliance management, collaboration with governments, living
and working outside one's own native country, managing transnational
teams, negotiating across borders, multiple language capability, and understanding the external global environment. As can be interpreted, it would
seem that communication efficacy is intrinsic to each of these dimensions.
Interestingly, the survey found that *not one* of these dimensions was listed
among the top five in terms of importance or priority by any of the 1,500
respondents. The exception to this was responses by Japanese and Korean
managers (mid, not senior level); "having a global mindset" was listed as
important by this group. It seems that an enhanced understanding of the
prerequisites of becoming truly global will need to occur throughout all cultures before organizations can begin to realize the competitive advantages
of cultural sophistication. It would also seem critical for organizations to
reexamine what perspectives they hold as important or as priorities in light
of what they practice as they conduct day-to-day business in international
markets.

Beyond achieving enhanced levels of understanding, cultural savvy
has strong business implications. Behrman (1995) stated that the competitive
strategies of both governments and companies have not sufficiently taken
into account the cultural bases for the policies and strategies of others.
Further, he stated, "the nature and extent of the similarities and differences
among countries are culture based and must be understood if the world is to
be served by a system of cooperative competition" (p. 2).

Certainly, cultural communication contrasts range from language
issues (both nationalistic and functionally specific language parameters), to
interpersonal styles (personability and politeness), to norms (taking of
responsibility, change orientation). These varied dimensions underscore the
complexity and thus the challenge that cultural diversity presents organizations. We surmise the leading organizations have just scratched the surface
of what it means to be and act truly globally.

The Communication Diversity Challenge of the Future: Cognitive Diversity

Because the use of language and communication is a learned social behavior, the underlying meaning of the communication differs greatly from individual to individual. Beyond the gender, racial, age, and cultural diversity that exist in corporations, the diversity mosaic becomes more complex when we consider that each individual brings a significantly different style and cognitive orientation to the organization's communication landscape. We suggest that valuing and supporting this "diversity of the mind" is key to such critical organizational processes as creativity and innovation. Further, individuals who are considered on the "cutting edge" (now increasingly called the "bleeding edge" because of the formidable resistance such pioneers encounter) are usually those organizational players whose communication practices are dissonant, as compared with the prevailing adaptive culture. In other words, innovation occurs, in part, as a result of an individual or group of individuals having the courage to highlight their relative cognitive diversity.

Jenny Wade, Ph.D., a research scientist with a practitioner background in international corporate communications, has studied the phenomenon of divergent mindsets. The application of her findings led to the development of The Wade Mindsets Work Inventory, an assessment tool derived from developmental psychology and other related fields of inquiry that helps individuals understand the different ways people view their work environment, respond to it, and form differing patterns of perception called *mindsets*. A mindset remains stable over long periods of time and lends insight into how to approach people whose mindsets are different from yours in effective and constructive ways. The range of mindsets include the security, dominance, traditional, achievement, affiliative, and authentic mindsets.

Clearly, differing mindsets can impact the relative effectiveness of corporate communication, given the preferences each mindset holds. For example, if an individual holds a security mindset, he or she has a need to feel safe and secure at work and has a need for feeling that he or she belongs. As such, communication choices will probably be normative so as not to upset the desired stability in the communication environment. Thus, the communication choice may be more related to the sender's need for security than desire for efficacious communication.

Realistically, most organizations are light-years away from being able to value and integrate the formidable array of perspectives, opinions, and ideas that diverse minds bring to an organization. Valuing diversity of the mind has implications for the development of communication practices, especially as regards the ability of the players to enhance their sophistication around interpretation. Organizations that value and support cognitive diversity must have as its members skilled interpreters who can reach levels of understanding amongst diverse viewpoints without being derailed by the individual differences. That is not to say that diversity of the mind cannot be a critical goal to strive for; the achievement thereof holds the promise of greater creativity and innovation, and thus enhanced competitiveness. Of course, organizations must first pass the threshold of valuing more concrete elements of diversity, those of gender, race, age, and culture.

A somber statistic out of The Conference Board study (Troy, 1995) of 110 U.S. and 20 European firms highlights the relative maturity of organizations as regards diversity: 41 percent of the companies surveyed undertook work force diversity communication campaigns and none of these respondents claimed success in these initiatives, although 10 nominated it as an initiative they would like to redo. It order to be successful, respondents felt that the involvement of senior and line managers was critical. This may lend credence to the theory that diversity will not be taken seriously until the diverse populations themselves have reached positions of power and influence.

Certainly, electronic communication technology offers some relief from communication discrimination by reducing some of the diversity barriers and allowing for a more level playing field for all of the players in the corporate landscape. Still, as face to face and video-conferencing communication will continue to be important media for a variety of communication challenges, diversity will continue to be a critical force to be reckoned with.

Chapter 6

Reshaping the Boundaries Around Business

At its most basic level, the purpose of communication in the workplace is to provide employees with the information they need to do their jobs. At enhanced levels, communication can create understanding and make knowledge more productive. Organizations recognize the importance of being skilled at this competency, as according to the "1995 Industry Report" by *Training* magazine and Lakewood Research, 85 percent of the 1,803 companies participating in the study provide some type of communication skill development training (Lakewood Research, 1995).

However, as the discussion has described thus far, the workplace is undergoing continual, wrenching change that regularly challenges one's communication aptitude. This change is exacting its influence on every aspect of the organization: the way it is organized, the way its players communicate, and the context within which the communication is played out. Thus, organizational structure, behavior, and culture all present implications for communicating in the realm of constant change, requiring ever-more sophisticated levels of employee communication efficacy.

Effective organizations of the future will continue to adopt new, more fluid organizational structures to replace the traditional hierarchical structures that have dominated the business scene since the industrial revolution. These more fluid designs will increase the speed of information exchange and lower the barriers to change, providing the contextual environment within which the "future work" will be played out. Inherent in these fluid structures will be the presence of overwhelming levels of both ambiguity and opportunity.

The required roles and requisite behaviors of the future organizational players will continue to undergo transformation as well. Individuals will be expected to manage record levels of information and increasing project work, while being self-managing and solely responsible for their learning and development. The emphasis on collaboration will continue to dominate the scene, with fluid structures of expanding and contracting teams becoming the venue through which projects are designed, managed, and completed. The use of contingent workers will increase, adding both challenge and flexibility to staffing needs.

Organizational cultures of the future will shift as well, as rapid changes challenge the ability to have a consistently intact and defined culture. Both the core and contingent players of the future will be exposed to numerous and differing cultures on a regular basis and will have to be able to thrive within each of them. Interestingly, this shift toward multiple, and sometimes illogically paired, cultural artifacts will be occurring at a time when most organizations are just beginning to understand the impact of a singular dominant culture.

This future, as described, is not new to most managers. The literature is replete with futurist predictions of what the requisite organizational structures, behaviors, and environments will be. What has not been fully examined are the communication implications of these shifts. In essence, the "new responsibility" of both organizations and the individuals who work for them is grounded in the fact that the greatest challenge of the future will be to *understand* communication dynamics holistically and to *apply* this knowledge accordingly. The simple recognition that "communication is important" is not, and never has been, enough. Nor is "increased awareness" a legitimate measure of effectiveness for communication practices. Again, the power of communication lies in its ability to create understanding and to make knowledge more productive. Settling for "increased awareness" overlooks the potential of efficacious communication as a valuable competitive capability.

Companies of the future will be required to delve deeper into the human side of communication behavior and to factor these behaviors as heavily as financial factors are weighed today when designing communication strategies. Clearly, the most expert technological system and most brilliantly conceived communication campaign will fall short of its goals if individual and collective behavior are not understood. Finally, the responsibility for understanding this communication behavior will no longer fall solely on the shoulders of human resource and communication professionals. This responsibility is indeed "new" because it will apply to all employees, in all functions, at all levels, thus necessitating increased collaboration amongst organizational groups.

In this light, this chapter focuses on the critical characteristics of the three major influences that will most strongly impact internal corporate communication in the future:

1. Organizational structure
2. Employee communication and information processing behaviors
3. Organizational culture

Going with the Flow: Organization Design and Communication

Much discussion has focused on the issue of structure as a factor that influences an organization's relative effectiveness. The prevalence of restructuring activities as a core dimension of many competitive strategies is testimony to the perceived power of organizational structure. While some maintain that structure, in and of itself, does not determine an organization's relative effectiveness, others argue that structure imposes a critical dynamic on the core processes. For example, Archea argues, "The arrangement of the physical environment regulates the distribution of information upon which all interpersonal behavior depends" (Archea, 1977, p. 121).

According to Johnson, "Physical characteristics are among the most enduring in an organization, and particular activities can come to be associated with particular locations" (Johnson, 1992b, p. 191). An organization's structure, therefore, whether explicit or "virtual" is designed to impart order or rationale to the flow of activities within an organization. From this perspective, order implies a linear-progression approach to both work flow and its productivity counterpart, decision making. Order also implies a progression of rational steps to be followed or clear-cut depictions of the organization's reality. As such, this greatly sought-after clarity became the impetus for many of the restructurings and re-engineerings that have occurred throughout the last ten years. But with clarity, and thus productivity, as a goal, how successful were these restructurings in imparting understanding?

As ambiguity, rather than clarity, better defines the dominant characteristic of the new work environment, for all practical purposes the goal of being "orderly" may be an exercise in futility for organizations. On the other hand, with the barrage of such words as *chaos, turbulence,* and other change-infused vernacular, one might believe that structure has all been eradicated from the modern organization. For example, organizations are espousing the virtues of the "virtual" corporation as the answer to the barriers and limitations inherent in a hierarchical and overly structured organization, while theorists are studying the impact of enhancing an organization's relative "fluidity."

While we are moving in the right direction by examining more dynamic models of organizational structure, certainly, some semblance of structure and order still exists, and probably will for a very long time. If for no other reason, at this point in our corporate and individual evolution few individuals can work under purely chaotic conditions. Further, there is nothing inherently "wrong" or "right" about a particular type of organizational structure, which we believe further misled those organizations charging headlong into restructuring. While virtuosity may work well for a group of electronically networked consultants who are sharing client information, this structure would hardly translate well to a newly formed project team who needs to rehearse an important presentation.

What can be "right" or "wrong" about an organization's design is the pairing of a certain structural type with an organization's internal and external environment. Complementary pairings between structure and environment are particularly important during times of change, as it has been proposed that this is the most critical time for an organization to be "correctly bounded" (Lee, R.J., 1993). The boundaries created by structure play a critical role in change management. Boundaries are where change is most dramatically felt and where the conflict needs to be managed. Depending on the environmental context, organizations can function well with either highly bounded structures, in the case of relatively stable environments, or more fluid ones, which are required during times of major transition. Of course, a balance must be struck. Overbounded systems tend to be maladaptive, while unbounded ones tend to be confusing, discordant, and unmanageable (Lee, R.J., 1993).

In the context of organizational communication, the most effective structures would be those that are semipermeable, allowing control without constraint and flow without deluge. As is the case with microorganisms, the organization's environment continually tests the mechanism of the membrane, challenging the organism to respond in certain ways in order to survive. In the case of a relatively stable environment, organizations will find that they are in the best position to respond innovatively to communication challenges. One may then think that boundarilessness is the key to innovation, and thus competitiveness. But if this regulating boundary is eliminated altogether, managers are faced with a steep communication challenge as "unbounded systems don't hear well" (Lee, R.J., 1993, p. 498). On the other hand, if the organization finds itself in a change-infused environment, it will find itself responding adaptively to these same challenges. Responding adaptively is not necessarily the inferior approach if it allows the organization to remain "whole" throughout the transition process. This dynamic underscores one of the great challenges to innovation during times of rampant change.

It is important to understand the impact of structure on critical aspects of management, such as employee, customer, and supplier behaviors. If an organization has a grounded understanding of the effect of its particular organizational design on the resultant behavior of its members, it can then examine this effect vis-à-vis the strategic intent and mission of the organization. It is only then that it will find itself in a position to make informed decisions around the necessity for change or adaptation to a new structure, virtual or otherwise.

Corporate Communication: The Structure Behind the Structure

While organization charts and facility layouts depict one element of organizational structure, the communication matrix that underlies, supports, and ultimately defines this structure is the true measure that determines an organization's strength, longevity, and effectiveness. Communication structure can be viewed as the relatively stable configuration of communication relationships between entities within an organization (Johnson, 1992b) and, as such, is viewed as central to the organizing process. The critical role of communication is underscored by Schall (1983, p. 560), who highlighted that without communication "there would be no organizing or organization." Further, Weick (1987, pp. 97–98) noted, "Interpersonal communication is the essence of organization because it creates structures that then affect what else gets said and done and by whom . . . The structure themselves create additional resources for communication such as hierarchical levels, common tasks, exchangeable commodities, and negotiable dependencies."

This contextual approach to structure and communication has been adopted by other researchers (Orlikowski and Yates, 1994; Giddens, 1984), who view communication as an essential element in the ongoing organizing process through which social structures are produced, reproduced, and changed. But in reality communication, like space, is somewhat of an ephemeral concept, because it is not composed of substances but rather helps define relationships between them (Urry, 1985). This quality alone could help explain why defining the dynamics of corporate communication amidst change can be so elusive. If communication defines the relational "white space" between substances (e.g., positions or structures) and these substances are in constant flux or evolution, the pattern of space between and around them also shifts continually.

One way to better grasp this fluid influence is to examine its component parts. Organization communication structure can be defined by its five main dimensions (Johnson, 1992a): relationships, entities, contexts, configuration, and temporal stability. Each dimension impacts the relative effectiveness of communication with regard to the flow of information throughout the organization's communication structure. As these dimensions interact dynamically and continually during organization communication, it can be seen how complex efficacious communication becomes.

The use of communication technology influences and, in turn is influenced by, the five major dimensions of communication structure. Technology, in part, determines how employees position themselves vis-à-vis other employees. It provides employees with a map of coordinates in which to operate within a gradient with other employees. Technology also plays a key role in defining the integrated activities of the employees by creating the communication boundaries inherent in certain technological configurations. Thus, the importance of conducting a thorough needs assessment of relationships, entities, contexts, configuration, and temporal stability before selecting and introducing communication technology into a changing organizational environment becomes clear.

For managers interested in formally analyzing their organizational communication structure, four major approaches have been delineated in the literature: formal analysis, network analysis, communication gradients, and cultural analysis (For a more complete discussion of these approaches, see Johnson, 1992a). Network analysis is a very systematic means of examining the overall configuration of communication relationships, both formal and informal, within organizations and has been characterized as the most powerful approach. Network analysis offers the most complete picture and is best at capturing, in a sophisticated description, the overall pattern of communication relationships within an organization. In turn, these descriptions can be a powerful diagnostic tool for managers because this approach develops rich descriptions of individual didactic relationships and thus reveals the overall configuration of these linkages across an organization. These linkages usually arise out of technological imperatives, thus the manager can analyze both the human and technical interfaces of communication throughout his or her organization.

Communication Efficacy and Organizational Size

As the increasing prevalence of mergers and acquisitions results in the development of behemoth corporate entities, the interplay between effective communication and organizational size becomes a critical issue. The necessity for communication increases with organization size, and thus increasing size is associated with an increased frequency of communication (Bacharach and Aiken, 1977). Unfortunately, this increased frequency rarely correlates with enhanced effectiveness. Not surprisingly, employees of larger organizations are more likely to report that communications about changes in policies or procedures were less timely and less complete than those of smaller firms (Snyder and Morris, 1984). This would help explain the trend toward decentralization as a strategic restructuring tactic in the aftermath of a merger or acquisition.

Several studies have examined the perceived importance of written and oral communication skills and organization size. Roebuck et al. (1995) derived data from 610 full-time employees of companies ranging in size from fewer than 50 to over 1,000 employees, with respondents' jobs ranging from operative to executive levels. Strong support was found for the importance of written and oral communication skills for current job performance and job advancement. While no significant differences were seen in the perceived importance of oral communication to company size, employees of larger organizations perceived writing as more important to job advancement than employees in smaller organizations. Given the increased prevalence of geographically dispersed employees and the resultant reliance on keyboarding our communication, this importance of written communication efficacy will undoubtedly increase in the future.

The communication dilemmas caused by size may be taking their toll. In what looks like a case of "reverse synergy," Dunn & Bradstreet Corp., which in the past had been considered a model of similar entities supporting one another, is the latest company to abandon the "bigger is better" strategy in the name of shareholder value. After spending decades and millions of dollars shaping itself into a conglomerate of financial services and data, D&B now sees more opportunities and profits in breaking up into three entities, an information-services core, the Neilsen media-rating business, and a business that focuses on tracking consumer packaged-goods purchases (Gibson and Lohse, 1996).

Alliances

The formation of partnerships or alliances between firms is becoming an increasingly common way for firms to find and maintain competitive advantage. Certainly, telecommunication and information technologies are spawning both domestic and international business alliances not conceived of just a few short years ago. The New United Motor Manufacturing Company (NUMMI) is an example of a long-term strategic partnership created in 1984 between General Motors and Toyota. The alliance successfully introduced a new automobile production system into the United States and continues today as a model manufacturing organization (Levinson and Asahi, 1995).

Alliance structure, as well as success, differs greatly across the board. These partnerships, ranging from short-term virtual corporations to long-term strategic partnerships, rely greatly on effective communication practices. In fact, the employment of effective communication practices is one of the major differentiating factors. This would make sense as the very action of taking on an alliance partner permanently changes the communication structure of the existing organizations while creating new internal communication challenges for the newly created unit. Corporate alliances, like project teams, are based on the dynamics of relationship building and communication exchange. It would then seem prudent for organizations to examine "communication compatibility" along with other traditional due diligence factors when considering the development of alliance relationships.

Studies of business alliances have shown that "these sets of organizations, linked through formal collaboration, dramatically transform existing knowledge transfer patterns" (Levinson and Asahi, p. 50). Levinson and Asahi's report outlines both effective and ineffective communication behaviors of several alliances, including that of ten electric utility companies, now linked through the ATW Group, which we would consider as having strong communication compatibility. Before the alliance, these organizations did not exchange information on a regular basis, either amongst themselves or with software developers, on how they might, for example, handle EPA requirements. The alliance enabled the participants to create new formal and informal links for sharing information and communicating effectively in a timely manner.

A clear example of communication incompatibility is the failure of the Bell Atlantic/TCI proposed strategic alliance. While the CEOs of both corporations attributed the failure to constricting FCC regulations, an analysis of the information flow between the two companies reveals an absence of interorganizational learning. There was an absence of communication linkages at all levels, except for that at the very top, thus precluding an in-depth understanding of the proposed alliance partner.

Future Structures: Enter the Networked Organization

What was once considered critical to the management of power rolodexes and successful careers is now the activity considered critical to effective internal communication amidst rampant change, networking. The "network organization" (Bush and Frohman, 1991) is purposefully designed and thrives through a network of highly effective communicators who bridge, meld, and thus create synergy amongst the organizational units. Effective communication in change-infused cultures requires horizontal communication across departments and interorganizational boundaries at the peer level, directed to achieve innovation through concurrent involvement of functional specialists. In network organizations, horizontal communication not only predominates, it flourishes.

To be effective, "this process requires communication that is both simultaneous and spontaneous—simultaneous because individuals' actions are parallel and spontaneous because an understanding of what is required replaces the steady flow of directives from above. The result is interactive learning that covers technology, customer needs, distribution, financial strategies—in short, all of the elements needed to complete innovation" (Bush and Frohman, 1991, pp. 25–26).

The network organization's structure will comprise a hierarchical framework of functional specialists managed in traditional ways, overlain by temporary structures in which status and power are determined by one's ability to contribute rather than by one's position in hierarchy. What is key to this structure is the ability of networkers to become integrators of information not only from other members of a team or unit but also from others both inside and outside the organization. These networkers act as linking mechanisms that speed up the flow of information and help increase information processing capacity.

Instead of focusing solely on structural dimensions, the network organization depends on the behavior of individuals. The concept of the "gatekeeper role" helps shed light on this difference. The role of gatekeeper is likened to one of a funnel or channel between a body of expert knowledge lying outside the organization and the people within the organization who need to apply it. The gatekeeper responsibility is taken up by only a few individuals who are temperamentally suited for such an activity—a sparse network. Conversely, in a network organization management practices and climate assure that each individual feels the responsibility to be a gate-keeper by making it an intrinsic part of the job. Consequently, the liaison function becomes part of each person's job, rather than a role performed by designated individuals or groups. In this way, it is assured that formal vertical and informal lateral structure coexists across all units and levels, thus increasing the likelihood of creating understanding and making knowledge more productive.

In a similar light, Tom Peters (1992) describes the "new economy" as one where work will be "brainwork" performed by small semipermanent networks of autonomous project-oriented teams operating under the demands of speed and flexibility. An integral part of this "brainwork" will be this networking approach to communication, as he states, ". . . everyone has to be able to talk with, work with, everyone else. . . . The web of relations is the firm" (Peters, 1992, p. 181).

Early field research into this emerging structure finds support for its use. A natural study by Lee (1994) found that job performance of engineers was related to the *pattern* of work-related communication, not the total number of contacts or other traditional structural dimensions. Specifically, high-performance new engineers were integrated more broadly into the interpersonal communication networks than low-performance new engineers.

While the network structure holds great promise for enhancing organizational information processing and communication sophistication, the transformation to this new structure will be wrought with challenge. We have already begun to experience one dynamic of the emerging network structure with increased reliance on telecommuting. To this point, the following commentary is offered by Art Sherwood, a semiretired independent contractor to Los Alamos National Lab's (LANL) Technology Transfer Division, who speaks of his experience with telecommuting and navigating the new landscape:

> In my experience it's not working out so great, all this telecommuting. You miss out on the little day by day things that happen, like what gets said around the water cooler. You miss the satisfaction of working with others. You don't get to read body language or facial expressions when you receive e-mail.
>
> When I used to take a break at LANL, I'd often wander down the hall and interact with others. This sometimes produced the most productive results of anything I could do. At the very least I continued to build bridges of trust and

good working relationships with others. Here at home I'll go do a chore out in the yard, or flip on the TV to take a break. Nothing synergistic ever comes out of that perspective.

The Corporate Manager as a Network Communicator: New Roles, New Rules, New Responsibilities

There are two kinds of salespersons. The first, the order taker, passively fills the customers' stated requests. This person is not likely to realize much success or longevity in sales. A second kind of salesperson takes salesmanship a step further. This person knows how to recognize and tries to fill a customer's unstated needs and requirements, and considers the question, "Which of my products best fulfills this customer's needs?" This person also recognizes that for a product to be sold, it is necessary that the customer's needs and wants be defined, the product's characteristics be explained, the customer's objections be brought out into the open and answered, the customer be committed to accepting the product, and the product be delivered to the place and at the time the customer has specified.

This person increases his or her chances for sales, and hence commissions, by doing some homework because he or she is, in a sense, serving the customer as a consultant. The corporate manager as corporate communicator can likewise serve as a consultant. But what does it mean to be a communications consultant within the corporation? And why is it important that a manager adhere to a consulting approach?

As we have discussed earlier, the corporation's role, style, structure, and external and internal interactions are in a period of great flux. The corporate communicator—whether he or she or management is yet aware of it—has been thrust into a key position in the corporation, with great power to help or hinder the organization. The manager qua corporate communicator is becoming the central player in a radial version of the old parlor game "telephone." The fun of the game is to see how garbled a simple message could become being passed linearly through a large group of people. In this radial version, the communicator is called upon to "pass the message" from management to employees, from inside to outside, from the sales manager to the salesman, etc. If the communicator simply repeats the message, without any errors in style or content, he or she could be replaced by a parrot. The corporate communicator as consultant, however, is alert to the needs of the audiences served, and aware, too, of the foibles of the originators of the messages.

Finally, the communicator must be aware of the overall context of the messages, namely, the overall needs of the corporation. Take the example of a producer/director in a corporate media department faced with a client who wants to produce a training program. The client has a predetermined idea of what is needed, how the script should be written, how the program should be produced, who should be in the program, and so on. The communicator who passively accepts the client's notions of how things should be done is an order taker; the communicator who takes time to analyze the problem has a better chance of selling the client the appropriate product.

All too often the client has not adequately or correctly defined the communications problem. In this case no appropriate solution can be determined! The communicator's role as a consultant in today's corporate environment involves answering a series of questions, namely:

1. Is there a communications problem?
2. What are the objectives of the communication?
3. How should the results of the communication be measured against the objectives?
4. What is the profile of the intended audience?
5. Where is the intended audience and in what environment will it receive the communication?
6. Will a formal communication prove cost effective?
7. What medium (or media) will be the most communications effective?
8. How will the program be produced?
9. Did the communication succeed or fail, and why?

By answering these questions a communicator can help lay the foundation for a successful communications program. Moreover, the communicator/consultant has a unique opportunity to contribute to the management of solving the corporation's problems. Without the role of consultant, then, a communicator runs the risk of creating programs that do not produce results; and no amount of clear language, sparkling visuals, or sophisticated production techniques will serve if the communicator does not solve the right problem, for the right audience, using appropriate language, in a cost-effective medium. This means that, as well as creative production talent and skills, the communications professional must have expertise in analysis and insight into marketing, sales, personnel functions, organization theory, management information systems, accounting, and psychology, among other disciplines. Without some grounding in these disciplines, a communications professional can only help the client halfway. As a consultant, the communications professional needs to take a hybrid, interdisciplinary approach to the business of solving communications problems.

It no longer suffices for the communications professional to rely solely on a "specialty" (e.g., writing press releases, designing graphics, producing a video program); he or she must be aware of the gestalt in which he or she operates. Assume, for example, that a media producer/director has been asked to develop a training program on the use of a new computer system. In order for effective communications to take place, the communications professional must have an adequate understanding of the basic operation of the computer, how the computer system interfaces with other aspects of the company's operations, what the short- and long-range effects of the installation of the computer system will be on the company personnel and the company's operations, how marketing operations may or may not be affected, and so on. It is not enough that the communications professional develop a clear picture of the computer system's function and operation; what must also be understood is that the advent of the new system will create changes not only for the corporation, but also for the personnel who will use the system. From this examination of the dynamics involved in producing this hypothetical training program, it will be seen that the communicator must have an understanding of the computer system itself, the context in which the system will be used, the psychology of change, the perceptions of the personnel who will ultimately have to use the system, and how the corporation's internal and marketing operations will be affected by the introduction of the system. Without this view of the context in which the system will be installed, the communicator will create a training program in a vacuum. This systems view of the corporate universe in which the training program is produced runs parallel to the metamorphosis of hybrid disciplines now emerging in many corporations.

This phenomenon seems likely to continue. As pointed out over 21 years ago by the Institute of Life Insurance in its fall 1975 Trend Analysis Program Report, one of the trends of the future will be the development of "New corporate disciplines, or reorientation of established ones, such as actuaries in personnel departments, social scientists in long-range planning, and political scientists in investment departments." While this does not imply that company publication editors will eventually become video engineers, or vice versa, it does mean that communications professionals will need to have an overall understanding of the corporation and an awareness of how individual communications problems and their solutions relate to these various functions.

This hybridization is especially pertinent with respect to training activities. It bears repeating, for example, that those in training functions, while expert in training systems and development, are usually not expert at translating training content into a media program (especially if the medium is not print). Media producers, on the other hand, are more often than not unfamiliar with training principles and techniques. This is obviously not a viable situation for the corporation. Communications technology has shrunk the globe. It no longer matters that distance separates corporate divisions because communications technology can connect them. Communications technology has fostered the broadening scope of the corporation as an entity and sustains its activities. Technology—communications technology in particular—has created change with escalating effect. The role of the manager qua corporate communicator has become one of helping the corporation to adjust to this change by creating understanding and making knowledge more productive.

Bringing Who You Are to What You Do: Communication Behaviors in Organizations

In general, human beings are imperfect communicators (Scully, 1995). This fact stands in stark contrast to the fact that effective communication skills are becoming increasingly important in a variety of occupations, with a recent study delineating 10,000 job positions that requested communication skills as a key prerequisite (Casady and Wayne, 1993). Communication competencies have been found to be strongly related to supervisory perceptions of overall subordinate job performance (Scudder and Guinan, 1989), and these competencies have been found to be key factors in entry-level business jobs and subsequent success on the job (Curtis, Winsor, and Stephens, 1989). Communication efficacy has been consistently identified by chief executive officers, middle managers, first-level managers, and deans of business schools as important for business success and professional advancement (Andrews and Baird, 1986; Bennett and Olney, 1986; Harper, 1987; Porter and McKibbin, 1988).

Because of individual information screens and mental models developed through gender-based, cultural, educational, and business experience–related differences, we each hold unique perceptions and interpretations of information. This leads to the communication of ideas, thoughts, and questions that are not interpreted by the receiver in the fashion that the sender intended. While on one level such diversity in communication orientation brings fresh perspectives and creative ways of interpreting information, on another level such disparity amongst individuals in an organization can render communication completely ineffective. Insight into communication behavior can help managers better understand effective and ineffective applications of communication at the individual level, which in turn affects the larger system.

Media Richness

The Media Richness Model of media choice in organizations helps lend insight into individual communication behavior. The model focuses on ambiguity as the pivotal attribute in understanding communication activity and identifies ambiguity reduction mechanisms employed by organizations to cope with this ambiguity. The concept was proposed by Daft and Lengel (1984, 1986) and asserts that communication media can be arrayed along a continuum of media "richness" based on differing capacities to resolve ambiguity. Relative media richness is defined through four criteria:

1. Speed of feedback
2. Variety of communication channels employed
3. Personalness of source
4. Richness of language used

On the continuum, face-to-face communication is the richest communication medium, followed by videoconferencing, telephone, electronic print media, and finally nonelectronic print media. The model proposes that, given the ambiguity level of the task at hand, individuals choose communication media whose richness best matches that level. In a revised version of this model, Daft, Lengel, and Trevino (1987) looked to the Theory of Structural Symbolic Interactionism (Stryker and Statham, 1985). This theory states that interpersonal interactions are symbolic because individuals use interactions as a basis for constructing meaning. Thus, the revised media-richness model proposes that certain media carry symbolic meaning that transcends the explicit message. By implying that symbolic meanings play a part in choosing communication media, the behavior is depicted as less rational and thus perhaps matching of task and media richness is not thought to occur in some situations. Of course, rational matching has three situational constraints, which prevent communicators from being able to employ the richest (and thus most appropriate) media:

1. Geographic separation of communication partners
2. Pressures emanating from the task
3. Unavailability of critical mass communication partners in computer-based networks

Studies on the practical application of Media Richness Theory have shown that high-performing managers are more media sensitive than low-performing managers (Daft, Lengel, and Trevino, 1987). In other words, high-performing managers are more likely to match media richness to communication task ambiguity, thus resulting in higher communication effectiveness. A meta-analysis of 40 early media studies lends further credence to the model (Rice and Shook, 1989). This study showed that higher level managers, who presumably have more ambiguous tasks, more frequently used face-to-face communication, while lower level managers more frequently used the telephone and written media. Jones et al. (1988–89) also reported heavy use of rich media by upper versus middle managers. Overall, studies have supported the model, although more so for traditional media over electronic media.

Based on their work with the Media Richness Model, Lengel and Daft (1986), provide six prescriptions for practicing managers:

1. Send nonroutine and difficult communications through a rich medium, such as face to face.
2. Send routine, simple communication through a lean medium, such as a memo.
3. Use rich media, such as discussions and meetings, to make your presence felt throughout the organization.
4. Use rich media for implementing company strategy.

5. Use multiple media on critical issues to make sure your message is heard correctly.
6. Evaluate new technologies critically rather than assuming that they are appropriate for the entire range of managerial tasks.

Behavior reflective of the media-richness theory research is beginning to evolve in practice. For example, with the increased complexity of business has come an increase in domestic travel by those at the higher levels within the organization. In 1995, for the first time, most domestic travel was done by organizational members who make more than $50,000 annually. Furthermore, the percentage of those travelers with incomes above $100,000 doubled to nearly 20 percent of travelers (Quintanilla, 1995). This shift illustrates how the day-to-day priorities of top management are changing, with an increased importance being ascribed to face-to-face communication and relationship building. Certainly, some of this travel is being taken on because the middle mangers who used to conduct the bulk of the travel simply aren't represented in the organization as they used to be. Quintanilla (1995) outlines how the vice president of corporate affairs for Kraft General Foods saw his staff cut by one third over the past five years, while his own travel jumped 25 percent in 1995. Given the highly competitive nature of global business, it is not surprising to find executives choosing the richest medium available to them when making an impact is their ultimate goal.

Social Influence Model of Technology Use

Communication is the fundamental activity through which social interaction is accomplished. In turn, communication is powerfully shaped by social processes such as sponsorship, socialization, and social control. Beyond examining individual selection of communication media, researchers have also studied the social dynamic of technology use in organizations.

The Social Influence Model of Technology Use proposes that perceptions of electronic media vary across individuals and that these media perceptions (such as richness) are, in part, socially constructed. To this end, four forms of social influence have been delineated that are believed to impact employees' perceptions and ultimate use of communication media. These influences are as follows:

1. Direct statements by coworkers in the workplace
2. Vicarious learning
3. Norms for how media should be evaluated and used
4. Social definitions of rational matching of media and ambiguity

Essentially, these influences indicate that because work groups are important sources of social support and regular interaction, there will be similar patterns of media use within groups and different patterns of media use across groups. Managers looking to align communication behaviors across organizational areas should consider the social influences at play within each area before mandating that certain communication media are used. The retrofit of technology onto individuals within organizations without consideration of prevailing communication behaviors, while quite commonplace, greatly reduces the organization's ability to harness the power of effective communication.

In this light, the Social Influence Model of Technology Use holds several communication implications for practicing managers, as delineated by Fulk and Boyd (1991):

1. Consider the receiver of your message. Some individuals are most attentive to communication put in writing, while others give more credence to face-to-face communication.
2. Think carefully about organizational norms regarding what should be formalized through written communication and what tasks can be accomplished verbally.
3. When introducing new communication systems into an organization, recognize that how individuals perceive and use them will not simply be a function of the technology itself. More pointedly, how it is evaluated in the social system will impact perception and use.
4. Media use is strongly influenced by organizational policies (e.g., budget) and managerial pressures (e.g., working styles).

Communication has been shown to enhance group effectiveness, including its role in limiting the deleterious effects of a phenomenon known as *social dilemmas*. A social dilemma is a situation in which members of a group are faced with a conflict between maximizing personal interests and maximizing collective interests. Communication among the members of a group has been shown to enhance cooperation (to maximize group interests). Studies have found that if members are allowed the opportunity to communicate their intentions prior to their actual decision, cooperation rate amongst members will be increased (Chen and Komorita, 1994). The increase of both diversity and uncertainty in the new corporate landscape increases the likelihood that employees will focus on maximizing personal interests. The intelligent use of communication within organizations can help offset the deleterious effects of ignoring the collective interests and can enhance the effectiveness of the growing number of project teams relied upon to get work done in organizations.

Communication and Information Overload

For all of the references to the prevalence of "information overload" in the Information Society within which we live, little attention has been given to its role in psychological burnout. As one might expect, individual information processing and communication behaviors have been shown to be adversely impacted by organizational stressors that lead to burnout. Certainly, managing the daily deluge of information, with its inherent communication challenges, becomes a significant organizational stressor for most mangers and executives.

Lee and Ashford (1991) examined the role played in managerial burnout by organizational structure and processes, notably work-unit standardization, formalization, and communication. Results from the research confirmed that the effects of organizational structure and communication processes on burnout were mediated by job-related stressors. In other words, while macroissues such as organizational communication structure impact individuals, they are at least partially mediated by microissues, such as the affective variable of burnout.

Further, under the increased pressure that precedes burnout, daily interpersonal relations between coworkers can break down, eroding trust and respect. In this scenario, communications become nonresponsive, negative, or reactive (Amour, 1995). Thus, in order to fully understand systemwide communication effectiveness, one must examine the presence of burnout as a mediating variable that could very likely render seemingly well-thought-out processes ineffective.

The New Responsibilities of Communicating in the Future

In addition to the myriad behavioral aspects that underlie routine interpersonal communication, effective communication practices in the organization of the future will demand even greater levels of challenge of the individual. Effective communication will require embracing new responsibilities, such as continual learning and development, resiliency, and tolerance of ambiguity. When communicating in a vertically focused network environment, the following competencies will be crucial (Bush and Frohman, 1991):

- Bridging vocabulary differences: This will include both culturally and functionally related differences in vocabulary.
- Learning and understanding new frames of reference.
- Interfacing with different people.
- Collaborating with people whose short-term goals differ from yours.
- Going outside one's area of expertise.

Organizations that integrate increasing amounts of vertical communication will certainly be met with resistance. As can be seen from the above list, the demands of the new world of corporate communication are much deeper than a lesson in skill building. Effective communication in such an organization is psychologically demanding in that it threatens our very orientation to giving and receiving information, and requires us to purposefully put ourselves in positions that are beyond "stretch," that are downright uncomfortable. On one level, this new orientation provides unlimited opportunities for learning and developing our communication efficacy. On another level, its demands will be so great that many individuals will not be able to embrace the new orientation without a tremendous amount of support and reward for taking the psychological risks inherent in the process.

Gilette's experience with instituting "networkers" showed that networkers who receive no reinforcement soon become ineffective (Bush and Frohman, 1991). Thus, as employees step up to the new communication challenges, organizations that wish to see them successful must provide the support required of such an undertaking. The first step, we suggest, begins with the modeling of these new behaviors by those individuals who possess the highest levels of influence within the given organization. Beyond this point, providing developmental opportunities that allow employees to enhance these competencies, as well as furnishing regular feedback on their perceived effectiveness, will become a critical responsibility of network organizations.

The Way Things Are Done Around Here: Organizational Culture and Communication

Each organizational has its own distinct values, behaviors, characteristics, and culture that influence individual expectations and behavior. Interpersonal communication systems are shaped by cultural values in line with traditional patterns of communication in the larger society. "This congruence intensifies the smooth flow of information with two important consequences: on the motivational level, sharing of common values makes for better consensus and commitment to those values; on the cognitive level, sharing of knowledge, ideas, and information enhances the level of productivity and innovation" (Erez, 1992, p. 43). As globalization increases, and the lines of distinction between cultural "societies" blur, the impact of the organizational culture will enhance and thus be looked to for cues in communication congruence.

Brown and Starkey (1994) elucidate the important relationship between culture and communication as follows: ". . . our conception of culture as a living metaphor to understand organizational behavior and events and our notion of communication as a symbolic form or cultural product are inextricably bound. On the one hand, culture is a product of social interaction mediated through communicative acts, and on the other, communication is a cultural artifact through which organizational actors come to understand their organization and their role within it." Thus, the importance of examining dynamics linked to organizational culture in the context of communication and change becomes clear.

In the following sections we examine four cultural dimensions that we feel exact an important influence on an organization's relative communication efficacy during times of rampant change: the priority of learning, the use of metaphor, the use of emotion, and the importance afforded status and power. We conclude this section with a discussion of communication amidst an extreme form of change, that is, communication characterized as crisis driven.

The Learning Organization

In times of change, it is insufficient to be motivated to the right thing; one must also be able. Thus, learning plays a powerful role in enabling organizations to embrace effective communication best practices during times of transitions. Because barriers to information flow are probably the greatest inhibitor to organizational learning, communication practices necessarily impact and are impacted by the organization's propensity toward learning. Organizational reflection and learning have long been recognized as an important means of promoting organizational change (Nicolini and Meznar, 1995).

In turn, constant change presents an exceptional challenge to learning, as we have traditionally viewed the process. For example, how can we learn when the text continually changes? Rote memorization of processes or reliance on heuristics bespeaks reactionary approaches to learning. Change requires proactive and integrative learning, which relies not on rules but on understanding how knowledge can be applied given situational cues. From this perspective, the concept of the learning organization, or an organization whose culture values learning and development of its members to the extent that the entire organizational organism "learns," has developed. From a managerial perspective, learning capability is "the capacity of managers within an organization to generate and generalize ideas with impact" (Ulrich, Glinow, and Jick, 1993). The concept of organizational learning and learning capability is still evolving, and as such most organizations are still in their infancy as regards their understanding of this phenomenon. As Nicolini and Meznar (1995) have noted, "To the extent that organizations continuously act and enact their environments, cognitive processes associated with learning continually take place whether the organization recognizes it or not."

In this light, we suggest that *reflection on learnings*, whenever possible, will enhance an organization's ability to understand its chosen communication strategies and to revise them in light of what they have learned. A simple and effective way for organizations to "learn to learn" is by taking the time to formally review "what are our learnings from this project?" This exercise can bolster an organization's communication sophistication by documenting, for example:

1. What was effective?
2. What was ineffective?
3. Why do we think what happened, happened?
4. What should we do differently next time?
5. How might we enhance our understanding of "effectiveness"?
6. Who might be able to help us enhance this understanding?

By examining how the group might reduce the barriers and enhance the facilitators of effective communication on future projects, the organization has "learned," and thus has risen one notch in terms of competitiveness.

Because of the rapid changes occurring within the corporate landscape, another dimension of learning that will become critical in the future is unlearning and relearning. It has been surmised that an organization that keeps repeating mistakes has failed to learn because of an inability to unlearn a set of processes that had been in place for some extended period of time. Additionally, once the organization breaks away from antiquated behaviors, it must relearn how to approach the process, given the myriad of changes that impact it in the current environment. As regards the increasing complexity of achieving communication efficacy, relearning in the future will comprise much more than the requisite refresher courses or review materials. Relearning speaks to our ability to learn how to learn all over again, given the opportunities presented to us, the particular climate for learning we find ourselves in, and our individual reception to learning at a given time.

For example, take the case of a manager who for an extended period of time has worked in a traditional fashion with his direct reports, that is, the employees were based in the same geographic location that he was, he held weekly face-to-face meetings in order to get progress reports, and his staff was predominantly white middle-aged men. Consider the steep communication learning curve this manager now encounters in the organization of the future: Not only must he unlearn internalized communication practice, but he must then relearn the practices that will characterize the future organization. He must manage and communicate across physical boundaries, he must utilize "less rich" communication channels, he must learn to receive and integrate new information continuously, and he must learn about the effects of diversity on communication. As such, in the future unlearning and relearning will probably challenge working adults to a greater degree than any other change-management skill.

A concept closely related to learning in organizations is that of organizational memory. Organizational memory concerns the knowledge base of the organization and the attendant processes that change and modify the base over time. Organizational memory is defined as the means by which knowledge from the past is brought to bear on present activities, thus resulting in higher or lower levels of organizational effectiveness. Beyond having a recognition of learning, an organization that shares and internalizes those learnings are more apt to maintain a healthy and effective organizational memory. Organizations that do not maintain such a memory have been described as having organizational amnesia. As such, challenges are taken on without the proactive integration of past knowledge and experience. An example of organizational amnesia in action is the continuation of downsizing practices despite the fact that previous restructurings did not yield the business objectives intended.

To the extent that organizational knowledge is consonant with the goals of the organization, organizational memory can be said to contribute to organizational effectiveness. Conversely, memory can be a constraint that threatens the viability of the organization and its ability to break free of ineffective patterns of activity. Organizational members must determine how best to apply past as well as newly acquired knowledge in order to meet the incompatible needs of flexibility and stability.

Metaphor

Another dynamic intrinsic to change-infused cultures is the use of metaphor in the predominant organizational vocabulary. Metaphors are used by organizational members to characterize their employing firm and to filter their experience in them. Thus, metaphors become an important source of diagnostic information for management who wish to better understand the prevailing cultural perceptions.

Studies using this linguistic technique have found metaphors to constitute a powerful communication tool that influences the structure of employees' thoughts and job performance (Palmer and Lundberg, 1995). Taken collectively, these metaphors can also reveal hints at the prevailing culture within an organization by the relative affective character of the communicated metaphor. For example, in an exploratory study of 401 hospitality employees, Palmer and Lundberg (1995) assigned the gleaned metaphors to one of eighteen different groupings that fell into one of seven overall categories relating to such factors as management skills, organization structure, operations, and power concerns. The researchers found twice as many negative metaphors as positive metaphors and about one third of the negative metaphors related to organizational structure and its inherent barriers to communication. Additionally, long-term, male, and managerial employees were found to more likely to hold negative metaphors. This is not surprising, as this population has probably been most adversely affected by downsizing and other climatic forces impacting organizations today.

Metaphors also aid in increasing clarity around complex organizational issues, and thus their use is increasing within internal corporate communication. Examples of this technique can be found in formal channels such as mission statements, values statements, executive speeches, and presentations, as well as in informal communication between employees as they work to better understand the increasing complexity of life within organizations. Probably the most prevalent use of metaphor within organizations today and of the future will focus on the definition and redefinition of change as it relates to that particular organization. For example, the intricacies of managing turbulent organizational environments have been described as similar to "navigating permanent white water" (Vaill, 1989).

With an eye towards the increasing diversity of the workforce, organizational communicators should be sensitive to shifts that must occur in the language of metaphors. For example, it may be ineffective to use metaphors that do not "speak" to particular audiences, such as sports, war, and other "masculine" metaphors in an increasingly "feminine" corporate landscape. Furthermore, attention should be paid to the type of change that is being communicated and the metaphors selected to enhance understanding.

In his work on the use of "metaphors of change," Robert Marshak (1993) defines four types of metaphors prevalent in organizational communication in the context of the type of change being described: fix and maintain metaphors, developmental metaphors, transitional metaphors, and transformational metaphors. Fix and maintain imagery implies that change was a result of something being broken. Thus, response to the change and the language surrounding the action is that it must be fixed and maintained. For example, "Things just aren't in sync. Find someone with a good set of tools fast!" Developmental change imagery implies building on the past, thus leading to better performance over time. For example, "We can do better than we have been doing. Find someone who can help build us into a better team!" Transitional change metaphors imply a move from one state to another. For example, "We've got to keep moving. We've got a long way to go, so we better start now. Find someone who's been down this road before to help us plan how to get there!" Transformational change metaphors imply a transfiguration from one state to a fundamentally different state. For example, "It's time we woke up to reality. Find someone who can help us create a new vision of the future, reinvent the organization, and get us out of the box we're in!"

Marshak (1993, p. 54) offers some guidelines to organizations who seek to better manage the metaphors of change and thus to enhance corporate communication during times of transition:

1. Listen to the word images you and others use to describe the change effort in order to assess clarity, consistency, and comprehension.
2. Make sure what you tell yourself and others metaphorically is what you mean literally.
3. Work to align the symbolic language system to help get people fixing, building, moving, or recreating in unison.
4. Seek to intentionally shape how people conceive and think about change through creative and constructive use of metaphors, images, and symbols.

5. When stuck, deliberately change the prevailing metaphor(s) and image(s) as a way to get out of the box and introduce new ways of thinking.

Emotion

Intricately linked to the use of metaphor is the use of emotion within organizational communication. The relative incidence of emotionally charged language is strongly linked to the norms of the prevailing organizational culture. Characteristically, formal organizational communication is often passionless and unemotional. This is what has made most such communication dull and unmoving for the audience it is trying to reach and, ultimately, to influence. Yet, the demands that change exacts on an organization's culture are extremely emotional, although often it is not introduced into the language of corporate communication.

Some researchers feel this must change (Nemee, 1995). In today's organizational climate of shrinking staffs, budgets, and a reordering of the very essence of work, people need to start acting, talking, and communicating with more emotion in order to make communication less psychologically illogical. For example, organizational leaders may want a culture that values teamwork, but they too often seek it by communicating dispassionately and individualistically. Alternately, leaders may also strive for a culture that values empowerment, but they do not nurture a culture that supports discussions around what it feels like when they are not feeling particularly powerful.

Electronic communication holds important implications for the use of emotion in corporate communication. On the one hand, the medium allows individuals who may otherwise feel uncomfortable with emotion to become a bit more expressive around their communications. Enhanced expressiveness can lead to enhanced understanding by those at the receiving end of the communication. On the other hand, electronic communication also allows for inappropriate bursts of negative emotion, labeled *flaming*. An increased incidence of flaming has been noted in several studies and, in part, implies a pent-up need for employees to be more expressive, especially during times of heightened uncertainty and change. We suggest that the use of more emotional language on the part of management could assist in factoring the human dimension into the change equation.

Electronic Media and Status

Another dynamic that exacts an influence on an organization's communication culture is the relative use of status and power by management. When electronic communication is introduced into a culture, not only do organizations sense an increase in process efficiency but also a change in the locus of knowledge. As "knowledge is power" to many managers and executives, this shift ushered in by electronic media equates to changing the locus of power, and thus status. For example, when information moves slowly, that is, physically, when Mohammed has to go to the mountain, or the courtiers to the court, those at the center of the information flow are in power. But when information moves at the speed of light, those in the so-called high places no longer can hold on to their status.

The impact of electronic media on status is highly articulated by Joshua Meyrowitz, Ph.D., in *No Sense of Place*. Although now eleven years old, Dr. Meyrowitz's examination of our electronic and social worlds puts in perspective what many executives and middle managers (and ex-executives and middle managers) already know—physical status is no armor against the onslaught of the flow of information electronically. Observes Meyrowitz:

> . . . for a hierarchy to exist, there must be more followers than leaders. In an era of easy and relatively shared access to information about people, one leader may be able to keep a close watch on thousands of followers, but thousands of followers can keep an even closer watch on one leader. The simply mathematics of hierarchy suggests the stronger likelihood of an undermining of the pyramid of status in an electronic age (p. 322).

Closer to the point, Meyrowitz explores the concept of authority when he observes, "Electronic media not only weaken authority by allowing those low on the ladder of hierarchy to gain access to much information, but also by allowing increased opportunities for the sharing of information horizontally. The telephone and computer, for example, allow people to communicate with each other without going 'through channels.' Such horizontal flow of information is another significant deterrent to totalitarian central leadership" (p. 322). To Meyrowitz's telephone and computer we can now add the Internet, the World Wide Web, and mobile telephony. As can be surmised, the status and power dimensions of organizational culture can be significantly altered through shifts in communication media and its composite practices. Thus, an organization's culture will determine, to a large extent, the organization's ability to harness the power of effective communication technologies.

Communicating Amidst Cultural Crisis

Crisis can exact a powerful impact on the relative stability of an organization's communication culture. Despite the fact these cultures tend to be enduring, crisis can cause dramatic mood swings within an organization's communication culture. For example, an organization whose communication culture tends toward openness can experience information meltdown during times of crisis. Why is this?

Kanter and her associates (1992) view crises as presenting both direct and indirect challenges to organizational leaders. Solving the problem inherent to the crisis itself is the direct challenge, while preventing the crisis from interfering with other aspects of the companies operations is the indirect challenge. Clearly, communication is the critical tool used to take on both the direct and indirect challenges presented by crisis. Effective communication practices during a crisis that address both cognitive needs (facts, data, analysis) and emotional needs (reassurance, sympathy, feeling of connection) have been credited with sustaining the lifeblood of organizations, such as was practiced by Burke of Johnson and Johnson during the Tylenol-tampering crisis (Kanter, Stein, and Jick, 1992).

But in doing so, the communication culture *itself* is affected by the crisis and presents a separate and more immediate challenge to leaders. If during a crisis an organization takes on communication activities that are not in concert with the prevailing culture, leaders have added to the confusion and rumor mills endemic to a crisis. Not recognizing this potential pitfall can exacerbate the crisis and render the organization incapable of emerging from the crisis intact.

For example, in a study of communication practices during a crisis-induced presidential departure at American University, Theus (1995) focused on the communication processes of interim leaders (the university's board) as they acquired power and selected strategies amid structural and cultural disarray. In short, increased uncertainty and heightened emotions caused the development of a power vacuum as interim leaders fought turf battles over access to and control over information. As a result, communication channels narrowed, leaving critical communication players, such as the public relations and student affairs executives, in the dark. One of the critical findings was that the board was not versed in the *values and norms* of the organization it attempted to direct, and, as a consequence, the actions of the board over the scope of the crisis were not perceived as culturally legitimate by insiders. This cultural disconnect made a strong impact, in part inducing several managers to resign, and the president who ultimately replaced the departed president resigned the post less than two years later.

Chapter 7

Harnessing the Power of Electronic Communication Technology

$\mathbf{F}$ace-to-face is still the best communication environment. After all this is how it started, with the members of our ancestral tribes sitting around the campfire telling stories of the day and the group. A May 1991 survey of 32,000 employees conducted by the International Association of Business Communicators (IABC) and Towers Perrin found that ". . . personal communication from an immediate supervisor or a senior executive in a small group setting is the preferred form of communication. Employees want to know that management cares about them and their concerns" (Matthes, pp. 3–4). In a separate study by the IABC and Johnson and Higgins, 92 percent of the CEOs surveyed cited personal and small-group meetings as the best method of communicating to employees.

These days, however, the organizational "tribe" has expanded to global proportions and electronic technology has likewise globally extended our ability to communicate. In effect, we have the ability to communicate face-to-face, but the "face" is mediated, that is, it is electronic in form.

Direct, personal communication notwithstanding, managers and employees have various forms of electronic media to facilitate the communication process: linear videotape, teleconferencing, multimedia (i.e., interactive videodisc and CD-ROM), the Internet (i.e., e-mail and the World Wide Web), and mobile telecommunications.

Linear Video

As Chapter 2 points out, videotape has been around since 1956 and in the nonbroadcast context since 1959. In effect, linear videotape has been used in the organizational context for over 36 years for a variety of purposes, including employee communications, employee news, management communications, role playing, skill training, and sales training. While certainly linear videotape has also been used for marketing, sales, and various external communications applications, it is the internal communications applications that concern us in this volume.

The Benefits for Employee and Management Communications

Since the late 1960s, managers and producers have given two central reasons for the use of videotape for employee communications—cost effectiveness and communications effectiveness. For example, users have indicated it costs too much, in time and money, to bring all managers and supervisors together at one location and that such meetings are not always practical. In other words, videotaped employee communications messages enable employees to participate in such meetings with executives from company headquarters, even though the experience is vicarious.

Company managements have expressed that videotaped messages give employees "a closer look at top executives"; "help relate field to home office"; "provide a good opportunity to get the whole picture"; "give an overall view that would otherwise be difficult to grasp." So strong is the feeling about videotape for employee communications that managers and employees have stated, "all corporate employees should be made to see the tapes"; "I had never seen an annual shareholders meeting before and found it interesting and informative"; "especially enjoyed pictures of other plants"; "employees would enjoy hearing more about the various products and companies"; "more on shares and stock for employees"; "will probably increase my savings and investment plan as a result of viewing the tapes."

In various ways, the benefits of using videotape for general employee communications are the same as those for management communications and marketing: Videotape has speed, credibility, immediacy; it brings the event, the person, the place to the employee. There are primarily two reasons why corporate managements have used television for employee news: communications effectiveness, and improved employee morale. The inherent technological and psychological characteristics of videotape and television allow corporate managements to communicate information in a way that is quite different from the content and style of the "print" employee news format. A statement from top management in video is a very different communications environment from the very same statement in print form. When the chief executive officer makes this statement on video, it is more alive, more direct, more personal, more credible. The television camera does not lie. It sees all. People "feel" people via television. Rightly or wrongly, television does communicate on an emotional, visceral level.

On the other hand, television is not very good at communicating details or facts that can be reviewed "at will." Home video and interactive videodiscs, notwithstanding, television (and hence, videotape) is not like a print piece, CD-ROM, or Internet website, which can be studied, analyzed, gestated, and reviewed at the viewers discretion. Thus, the perception of corporate users that video is more communications effective than print must be understood from the point of view that video does *some* things better than print, but the reverse is also true.

With respect to employee morale, the advent of employee news television programming parallels the development of other electronic communications devices that have permeated the corporate culture in the last two decades, the most prevalent of which is the computer. Others include greater use of telecommunications devices, for example, fax, teleconferencing, CD-ROM, and more recently, the Internet. Employee news television programming is but one example of the changes in employee–management relations in the last decade or so. It provides employees (at least ostensibly) with the view that there is a more "open" employee–management communications environment.

Using videotape for the distribution of management communications to an organizational network has several advantages. First, the medium has *speed*. Videotaped messages can be shot, edited, duplicated, and distributed in days to a domestic and/or international employee audience. This is not to say all programs produced at this rate of speed will have the professional look or depth of content of a "Nightline." There are differences in content, of course, and more importantly there are vast differences in the number of people working on "Nightline" and (potentially) on a management communications video; probably on the order of 50 to 1. Yet once a company has a video network in place, it can be an extremely effective and efficient means of distributing "messages" to employees, if need be.

Second, the video medium has *credibility*. Rightly or wrongly, television today is perceived as *the* medium for news. If you're seen on television you gain at least exposure, if not credibility. Today's communications environment virtually demands that executives use the television medium as one major means of communicating with employees. Executives may not be able to shake the hand of everyone in the organization, but video is "the next best thing." Third, videotape's look of *immediacy* gives the viewer the impression that the executive presentation is live, present, and directed at the viewer. Videotape gives an employee the feeling (whether real or not) that the executive is there, making a connection with the employee.

The Benefits for Employee and Management Training

Videotape has been used for a variety of training purposes, including role playing, skill training, and sales training. For example, managers, producers, and trainers have given four reasons for the use of videotape for role playing. Videotape:

- Allows trainee participation
- Simulates reality
- Saves time

When users indicate that videotape "allows trainee participation" they are alluding to videotape's ability to bring a trainee into a learning situation on a visceral as well as cognitive level. It is one thing for a trainer to "lecture" to a group of sales trainees; it is quite another for the trainee to be in the thick of the learning process, so to speak, with videotape.

With videotape a trainee becomes the "content" of the training environment. While there is a certain amount of product information to be learned in this kind of training situation, what is really being learned in a role-playing training environment is "interpersonal" skills. Translate interpersonal skills into "people" skills, dealing with emotional content, dealing with change. In a very meaningful sense, videotape allows trainee participation on the playback side of the process.

People watching people is one of the major conceptual pillars of "Candid Camera." So, too, with videotape and role playing, except there's a twist. In the organizational role playing context, people watch themselves. And while it is engaging and compelling, it can sometimes be painful. It follows that videotape in a role-playing training environment "simulates reality." One could easily substitute the term *role playing*. Trainees can simulate a sales context, for example, and play parts in order to feel their way through the situation. It is through feeling (1) the informational content and (2) the emotional context that the training is achieved. It is the combination of allowing trainee participation and the simulation of reality that gives videotape its cost effectiveness and efficiency, that is, "it saves time."

It stands to reason that if you rehearse a situation in advance, when you get to the situation you will perform better. It is like studying for a test, as opposed to waiting until you get to the test to figure out what to do. One of the major tenets in the media-relations arena is to come before the press with your content agenda *preplanned*. In other words, regardless of the questions asked, the executive answers with a preplanned text, rather than off-the-cuff. The former is more directed; the latter is potentially a public relations disaster. A sales situation further illustrates the point. If you have rehearsed your sales pitch, dealt with objections in advance, preplanned a smorgasbord of closings, the chances of getting the sale are much better than if the salesperson has not practiced.

It is similar with management–employee communications. In the last few years, as a direct result of mergers and acquisitions, foreign competition, the virtual globalization of many industries and markets, and new technologies, American corporations have gone through significant organizational changes, not the least of which is the apparent "flattening" of the organizational chart (which Chapter 3 has discussed in greater detail). As a result, many managers have had to learn how to deal with the fallout—people losing jobs; people changing jobs and careers; people learning new skills—in other words, people having to deal with change. Role-playing training (with videotape) has provided an environment in which managers can practice dealing with employees before having to deal with "the real thing."

Lastly, videotape has a major advantage with respect to the role-playing/training environment—its instant playback capability. Videotape's "magic" in the role-playing environment is its ability to be rewound and played back instantly for the trainee's edification. This characteristic and its effects can be extraordinary. We have often witnessed top level executives, perhaps first time video users, watch themselves on the playback of the first run-through of a presentation and give themselves a highly professional, on the mark critique of what was right and wrong about their on-camera appearance. Sometimes, they only need to see a few minutes to go through that internal reordering of perceptions critical to an executive's improved performance. Very often the producer or trainer doesn't need to say much. The trainee sees all he or she needs to see, all through the videotape medium.

There are six reasons why videotape works in the sales training environment:

1. It is communications effective.
2. It is cost effective.
3. It provides training uniformity.
4. It has the ability to reach a nationwide audience.
5. It is self-instruction capable.
6. It provides production flexibility.

By *communications effectiveness*, users have meant the video medium is the most real, the most present communications medium you can find—the closer you can get in the training situation to the real thing, the more potent your training will be. Users have also indicated that television demonstrates rather than merely announces, that the viewer concentrates more fully on the videotape's content because he or she is on a one-to-one basis with the communicator on the screen. The communicator has at his disposal all the impact tools of television—sight, color, credibility, intimacy close-ups of subject matter, animated illustrations, instant travel to distant places, and important people, etc.

In terms of *cost effectiveness*, if it were not for videotape technology, courses would require more instructors. Further, many sales trainers have experienced that when one considers salaries, lodging, and food, plus the expense of course materials, videotape technology can reduce training costs and time significantly. For example, under an old system one company brought some 700 salesmen to the home office for up to five weeks of training. Under a system using videotape, regional offices were equipped with video players and presentations were canned. The company projected savings of about $1.5 million over ten years! Another company observed video would enable them to make better use of the time spent in the class by entry-level account executives. It also projected a reduction in costs.

Sales training content conveyed via videotape provides a *uniformity of information and performance*. For example, in many instances sales-training videos involve role modeling—an exemplary sales technique or salesperson demonstrating a selling sequence. The videotape medium can capture the "best" salesperson or selling sequence for demonstration to other salespeople or sales trainees. In effect, the videotape precludes different trainers from demonstrating a range of sales techniques in terms of "performance" level. This uniformity (theoretically, at least) ensures a higher level of training uniformity in terms of training objectives.

The video medium provides *reach to a national and (in some cases) international sales training audience*. With the great accessibility to duplication facilities and use of satellites for the distribution of programming, companies can get their sales-training message out to a specific audience within days, if necessary, once program production has been completed.

In terms of *flexibility*, the durability of the technology is another inherent benefit of videotape in the sales-training environment. Cassettes are ideally suited for the rough-and-tumble handling that comes with use by many different individuals. Moreover, no operator is required, no darkened room. The salesperson, the training instructor, the "user," is in complete control. With the advent of 1/2-inch VHS players, the use of sales training videotapes is no longer confined to corporate headquarters, a regional training center, or the local sales office. The salesperson or trainee can now take the sales-training video home. This relatively new "playback" environment provides even greater scheduling flexibility. Because sales training demonstrations are produced collectively, these sales role-modeling videos can become a "library" of outstanding sales techniques and salespersons.

There are nine benefits for the use of videotape for skill-training purposes. They are:

1. Communications effective
2. Efficient and flexible to use
3. Able to manipulate real-time/real life while maintaining realism
4. Cost effective
5. More effective than print and other media

6. Able to reach decentralized audiences
7. Able to extend the subject expert
8. Uniform in instruction
9. Able to provide fast turnaround from production to distribution

Communications effective means that using videotape for skill-training purposes gets the message across, communicates content effectively, and helps get skill training results. For example, it has been shown that where the instructional task is to teach "motor skills" (i.e., as in a skill-training situation such as operating or performing maintenance on a machine), motion is helpful in the media presentation, especially if the information is not easily conveyed verbally or the trainees are unfamiliar with the task. This suggests that a videotape presentation would be more desirable for training purposes than a series of slides or a print workbook.

It could be inferred that the use of motion to teach a motor skill and, in turn, the use of videotape in this kind of training situation is the most logical choice because people are naturally imitative. This imitative process operates from birth. Studies have shown that babies imitate adult rhythms of speech through physical expression—movements of the hands, arms, feet, and head. This rhythmic, physical dance is clearly evidence in adults: pointing of a finger at the end of a sentence, shifting the body during conversational transitions, leaning forward for emphasis at the beginning of an important statement.

If one accepts the concept that imitating through demonstration is operating during the communications of motor skills, it follows that attitude/behavior change in a trainee can similarly be affected. Exposure to a role model (as in a supervisory training program. for example), can affect post-training behavior in several ways. The observer (trainee, salesperson, clerk) can (1) learn new behavior, (2) have already learned behavior facilitated (previously learned behavior responses are produced), or (3) have already learned behavior inhibited or disinhibited. Thus, where imitation is required—learning a motor skill, learning an attitude via a real-life demonstration or role models—videotape is an ideal medium for communications effectiveness.

Videotape also has the capability of reaching decentralized audiences. Clearly, with the advent of the helical-scan U-Matic format in the early 1970s, and subsequently the VHS format in the mid-1970s, it became very inexpensive and efficient to use videotape as a means of reaching corporate-wide audiences. Given this kind of distribution capability, videotape also has the advantage of extending subject experts. A major problem in corporate training is getting pertinent information to all those that have a need to know. Subject experts are just that. They are experts in a particular subject. They have a level of expertise that is not common in the organization. Therefore, what they have to say (due to either their training and experience, or both) is significant to those that could also benefit from the information. Unfortunately, many subject experts are terrible communicators. Moreover, even for those who are adequate communicators, they cannot be in all places to communicate their expertise on a timely basis. Enter videotape. In some cases, a subject expert's presentation will be merely recorded, duplicated, and distributed to all trainees throughout the corporation. The videotape medium is cost effective in this regard. More often (fortunately), a subject expert's videotaped presentation will form the basis for a more highly scripted, visualized, and better paced videotape that is properly shot, edited, and then distributed.

An ancillary benefit to this approach is that training information becomes more uniform. In other words, rather than depending completely on trainers with a range of competency to present more or less the same training content, the videotape training presentation can obviate some of the inequalities in the training environment. While the videotape presentation will not and cannot be the ultimate equalizer, it can help reduce some of the training quality inequalities that are bound to evidence themselves in a corporate training environment.

Teleconferencing, a.k.a. Business Television

An April 1995 study on telecommuting suggests that personality type, not technology, is the key factor in successful telecommuting. The study, based on in-depth reviews of corporations with telecommuting programs, indicates that an employee's personality type can predict his or her success as a telecommuter. The study also showed that companies without access to advanced technology such as videoconferencing do not need to delay starting telecommuting programs, which can be successful with more affordable tools, such as phone, fax, and computer communications.

These findings are from *The Telecommuting Handbook*, released April 1995 by the Electronic Messaging Association (EMA). The 75-page handbook was written for employers setting up telecommuting programs and for employees who are considering alternatives to going to the office five days a week. It provides a practical guide to employees considering telecommuting, including checklists for preparing a home for telecommuting and suggestions for gaining organizational approval. Case studies detail several corporate telecommuting programs, from selecting which positions and participants were eligible to participate to measuring changes in productivity. *The Telecommuting Handbook* was prepared for EMA by David A. Zimmer, principal of American Eagle Group, a market research firm based in Warrington, Pennsylvania.

Examples

The Postal Service established a satellite network in December 1990 to keep in touch with its enormous employee population of more than 750,000 employees. When postal rates increased in February 1991, it used the network to simultaneously train employees from 73 divisions about the implementation of the new rates (Matthes, 1991, p. 3).

Ball Aerospace Systems Group, a Colorado-based company that develops satellites and other aerospace systems for NASA, uses a quarterly television broadcast to communicate with its 3,000 employees spread out of over several locations. "Aeronews" was developed in response to a survey evaluating internal publications—employees wanted to learn more about what was going on in other departments and wanted more visuals (Matthes, 1991, p. 4).

In a collaborative linear-videotape and satellite communication effort, Dallas-based J.C. Penney's direct broadcast system was used in mid-September 1992 to air a DuPont-sponsored program on legwear fibers and styles. Sales associates in virtually all units were required to view the video. While it aired, each store taped the program. The video contained information that sales associates could then use to educate consumers and to make them aware of all the legwear options available (Reda, 1992, p. 69).

Teleconferencing is a generic form of pulling together various technologies and applications while using electronic channels to facilitate real-time communication among a group of people at various locations. Teleconferencing encompasses various subcategories, which include audioconferencing, audiographics conferencing, videoconferencing, business television, and distance learning or distance education. Audioconferencing employs the use of voice communications by the use of telephone lines.

Teleconferencing has clearly become an accepted means of business communication. Technological advancements coupled with inherent efficiencies will probably continue to spur the growth of teleconferencing; eventually it will become a household word, much like the telephone. The greatest change in the industry are the end users. Teleconferencing users were once solely Fortune 500 companies, which were in a position financially to purchase the necessary technology as well as to possess the expertise to use it. Today, users now cover virtually everyone, from the medical profession to business organizations. In the medical field, medical groups use audioconferencing to discuss patients and to obtain long-distance opinions of x-rays while using audiographics. Business organizations use audioconferencing to bring their executives together by phone.

Teleconferencing seems to work best when it fills some unique human need or a unique application. As a corollary, it is important, users say, to define that critical need. Further, teleconferencing managers need to take their "audiences" into consideration, in effect, to ask the question, "What are the audience's needs?" Paralleling this consideration are the requirements for a high degree of advance planning, rehearsal of teleconferencing participants, and high production values, particularly with respect to video teleconferences. Teleconferencing managers interviewed for *Winners! Producing Effective Electronic Media* (Marlow, 1994) also urge other users to make the content of teleconferences about "real people" and "real stories." In one instant, users are advised to develop systems that are "humanizing, require participation, provide feedback and have style." Finally, users are advised to create a conferencing system that has flexibility.

It is curious to observe that while teleconferencing deals with an electronic technology, the advice offered by users all centers on "people" considerations. While the users, for the most part, are concerned with the so-called software, or people elements of the technology, they are rarely concerned with the operational effectiveness of the technology. In effect, the technology appears to be transparent. And while users are certainly aware of technical considerations, their main production challenges center on human factors rather than technical factors. It is perhaps a sign of a technology coming of age that users are more concerned with human factors rather than technological factors. In the videotape technology arena, for example, in the 1960s technological problems were abundant, particularly with respect to technological standardization. It was not until the early 1970s, with the advent of the standardized and highly portable 3/4-inch U-Matic videocassette, commercially introduced by Sony, that videocassette technology took off.

According to several sources, in the 1980s teleconferencing was already beginning to take off as an internal and external communications tool as various corporate, medical, educational, and governmental institutions explored the possibilities of using it. In the 1990s, therefore, excellence is not as dependent on technological prowess as it is on managerial expertise and users' awareness of the technology's "people" communications potential. Further, the concept of teleconferencing, whether audio only or full-blown two-way video, two-way audio, is the expression of Marshall McLuhan's "global village concept" articulated in *Understanding Media: The Extensions of Man*. With the flowering of global telecommunications networks, the promise of networked multimedia communications, as John S. Mayo, President of AT&T Bell Laboratories put it (AT&T Bell Laboratories Technology Symposium, Toronto, Canada, October 13, 1993), is fast becoming a reality.

Trends in microelectronics, photonics, speech processing, video, computing, telecommunications and information-network architecture, wireless communications, software, and terminals are all creating vast opportunities for highly interactive information-sharing systems on a global basis. Ironically, these same electronic technologies will also have the effect of creating more "physical travel," what John Naisbitt refers to as "high tech/high touch." In other words, the more we gain capacity for traveling electronically, the more we desire to "press the flesh," so to speak.

Teleconferencing has the potential for encompassing all the other electronic technologies, at the office and in the home. The personal computer will become the central communication device. Sooner or later, it will all become standardized on a global basis, and highly portable. Dick Tracy's wristwatch will become a common technological reality!

Multimedia (Interactive Videodisc and CD-ROM)

CD-ROM stands for Compact Disc-Read Only Memory. Bergman and Moore point out, "Another factor has been the development of image-based applications that use graphic pictures and digital audio, and no motion video at all . . . The term 'multimedia' has been adapted as a generic reference to all such image-based applications" (Bergman and Moore, 1990, p. 5).

Thomas Reeves and Stephan Harmon, writing in the fall 1991 issue of *Interact, the Journal of the International Interactive Communications Society* (p. 29), take matters a step further when they define multimedia as ". . . an interactive database that allows users to access information in multiple forms, including text, graphics, video, and audio." They go on to define *hypermedia*, a subset of multimedia, as ". . . an interactive database that allows users to access multiple forms of information, but is specifically designed with linked nodes of information to allow that access in any manner of the users' choosing" (p. 29).

The Microsoft Corporation, in a February 1993 backgrounder, defines computer-based multimedia as ". . . the integration of text, graphics, audio, video and other types of information into a single seamless whole" (p. 2). Clearly, multimedia has evolved from an integration of various digital, electronic aural, and visual technologies into an interactive medium for use in the home and office. Multimedia (the simultaneous use of motion video, audio, and data, requiring the use of a computer, CD-ROM, and videodisc player) may be the future medium of choice if a CD-ROM product is distinguished by its accessibility, ease of use, and creative visualization.

There are two choices critical to creating a superior CD-ROM product:

1. An interface that makes a user's search intuitive.
2. A search engine (i.e., searching tool) that enables the user to get anywhere easily, to browse at will, and to find and aggregate information in anyway he or she desires.

It is the interface between the user and information on the CD-ROM that determines whether the user feels trapped inside a PC screen, and goes fleeing to the nearest book, or feels in control of searching through masses of material in a way that no print index can ever allow. If an electronic product does not make the search easy and effective, then it is little more than a method for saving library shelf space, and the user will soon determine that he or she is better off browsing through a book.

A search interface and engine also allow the user to:

- Browse the CD-ROM expertly.
- Browse a full-text article in the database.

- Copy information to a printer.
- Copy material to a disk.

According to Hank Evers of the Pioneer Corporation Multimedia System Division, multimedia's benefits have persuaded many print-based publishers to reevaluate their businesses. Publishers are learning to identify their business in terms of content (intellectual and artistic) that they own and to separate it from the medium in which it appears. This also holds true in network television. ABC News and the Discovery Channel find themselves in the same camp as *The Encyclopedia Britannica*—they are owners of content.

Why has multimedia technology, particularly CD-ROM, received wider acceptance, not only in educational and medical institutions but in a growing number of business organizations as well? Dataware Technologies perceives two reasons: "First, technological developments have substantially lowered the barriers to cost effective use of CD-ROM . . . A technology that was once only potentially beneficial is now affordable, easy to use, and widely employed. Second, CD-ROM has demonstrated clear benefits . . . Dataware points out that one CD-ROM can hold the equivalent of 1,500 floppy disks, 250,000 pages of text, or 12,000 scanned images at an incremental media cost of $2 per disc.

E-mail

Electronic mail (e-mail), the sending and receiving of electronic messages, is a major use of the Internet. E-mail is not only available from an account through an Internet Service Provider (ISP), but also through the commercial on-line services, such as America Online, CompuServe, and Prodigy.

The Benefits of E-mail

E-mail allows an individual within an organization to communicate electronically to anyone else in the organization, or, for that matter, with someone outside the organization. The communication flow can go from the so-called top of the organization to the bottom, laterally, or from the bottom of the organization to the so-called top. If an individual in an organization has access to e-mail, the opportunity for rapid exchange of information is enormous.

The organizational implications of e-mail with respect to manager–employee communications is equally enormous. To begin with, e-mail enhances the breakdown of the traditional bureaucratic/military organizational structure. Organizational members can communicate with each other directly, without need for an "intermediary." The speed and flexibility of e-mail transcends department boundaries, it allows people in an organization to communicate without great regard for so-called rank. This is not to say that politesse and respect for authority is out the window. But it does mean that an individual can communicate with another individual in an organization without depending on a supervisor to carry the message, or hoping that the secretary or assistant will deliver the message, or trusting that the internal mail system will get the "print" message to the other individual efficiently.

E-mail is, however, a nonsynchronous medium. Unlike a telephone conversation, in which the two parties (or three or more, if a conference call) communicate with each other simultaneously, with an e-mail communication (sent albeit at the speed of light), there is no guarantee the receiver of the message will be there when the message arrives; it may some time before the receiver of the message responds. However, the chances of a speedy interaction—whether via e-mail or by telephone, or fax—is enhanced by the fact that the e-mail can be composed and sent in relatively short order.

Angell and Heslop (1994, pp. 78–79) point to several other benefits of using e-mail in the organizational context:

It eliminates phone tag and improves response times.

It allows you to digest your messages and put more thought into your responses compared with using the phone.

It breaks down distance and time barriers of traditional written communications. You can send and read e-mail messages at any time, 24 hours a day, 365 days a year, for better communication across time zones.

It shortens the cycle of written communication. People can circumvent many of the inefficiencies of the office and the approval process of traditional paper-based communication.

It empowers the individual by flattening out corporate and sociological hierarchies and allowing for direct, interactive communication.

It improves productivity by speeding up the decision-making process by providing a forum for replies and clarifications.

It facilitates meeting planning and preparation.

It creates flexibility in the work day by reducing telephone interruptions, and it allows people to work from home or any other location with a computer.

It reduces postal and telephone charges.

An example of how organizations are using e-mail for internal communications follows:

Perot Systems Corporation, based in Dallas, publishes three online newsletters via e-mail. The internal communication department produces one every week and writes the others on an as-needed basis. Perot Systems chose this "low frills" approach for its simplicity and affordability. The department spends 15 hours a week collecting information. Copy approvals are completed within 24 hours, and the newsletters are distributed to its 2,400 associates (employees). The newsletters are typically no longer than three pages and include briefs about the latest company news.

(Miller, 1995, p. 23)

Netiquette

The inherent nature of e-mail also forces succinctness and directness. E-mail is not a medium that encourages long-windedness. It requires people to write messages that get to the point. Although it is certainly possible to send letters and memos of much greater length, an e-mail inherently requires brevity. This is probably because once an e-mail is composed, there is no need for printing it out, creating an envelope, putting on a stamp, getting it in the mail, waiting for the internal (or external) mail to do its work, and for the receiver to get it from their mailbox and read it.

For an excellent outline of network etiquette (Netiquette), the reader is referred to "Netiquette Guidelines" written by Sally Hambridge of the Intel Corporation. The document is published by the Internet Engineering Task Force's Responsible Use of the Network Working Group (www.cnri.reston.va.us). In the section devoted to one-to-one communication (which includes several dozen e-mail recommendations), Ms. Hambridge refers to such Netiquette guidelines as:

> Be sure to check with your employer about ownership of electronic mail.
>
> Respect the copyright material that you reproduce. If you are forwarding or reposting a message you've received, do not change the wording.
>
> Never send chain letters via electronic mail.
>
> Be conservative in what you send, liberal in what you receive.
>
> Make things easy for the recipient. Many mailers strip header information that includes your return address . . . be sure to include . . . with contact information.
>
> Know to whom you are sending.
>
> Don't send unsolicited mail asking for information to people whose names you might have seen on . . . mailing lists.

The Internet and the World Wide Web

There is abundant evidence that the Internet/World Wide Web is beyond a mere blip on the electronic media chart. It is real, it is growing in prevalence, and it is bound to become a major organizational tool in the form of an Intranet.

Intranets—defined as internal web servers used for specific tasks within an organization—are growing faster than the Internet according to preliminary statistics from International Data Group's research subsidiary, International Data Corporation (IDC). The number of Intranet servers now totals 70,000 (55 percent of total servers) and is expected to nearly triple in size in 1996 to more than 200,000, and to exceed 4.5 million by 2000. (PR NEWSWIRE, February 5, 1996). As recently as two years ago, Intranets virtually didn't exist. Yet now the market for internal Web servers—the hearts of corporate Intranets—is worth about $476 million, according to Zona Research, Inc. of Redwood City, California. Two thirds of all large companies either have an internal Web server installed or are considering installing one. Netscape already attributes more than half its revenue to customers building Intranets. Corporations' internal Web sites already outnumber their external ones. While exact figures are unavailable, industry analysts believe corporations will soon deploy 10 times as many internal Web servers as external ones. At IBM, the ratio has already hit 30 internal servers for every one external server according to comments posted to an online discussion group.

To draw a clear picture of the current impact of technology for employee communications, Cognitive Communications Inc. and The Document Company Xerox cosponsored a survey in the spring of 1996 of 731 corporate communicators, primarily from Fortune 500 corporations. Among the key findings of this survey, 95 percent felt that employee communications must take a key role in assisting their companies in technology upgrades. This is up from 79 percent in 1994. Another finding was that "The use of electronic media (e-mail, electronic newsletters, Intranets) for internal communications is overtaking print faster than expected." The report further states, "The overwhelming acceptance and expansion of e-mail within corporations in the last two years, coupled with the explosive growth of web technology, has made electronic communication the primary medium of choice for communications professionals at many corporations."

A broad range of other Internet examples abound—including Xerox, Sun Microsystems, US West, systems integrator Mitre Corp., consulting firm Booz-Allen & Hamilton Inc., IBM, USAA, MCI Communications, Sybase, Inc., Pan Canadian Petroleum, Chevron, Inc., Ford Motor Company, Federal Express, Visa International Inc., drugmaker Eli Lilly and Co., AT&T, Cadence Design Systems, Electronic Arts, Home Box Office, Douglas Aircraft Company, and Hewlett-Packard.

Joe Cahalan, Director of Corporate Communications and Public Relations at Xerox, lists three central ways the Intranet will change how companies operate (Ragan's *Intranet Report*):

1. It increases the ability to disseminate information: Employees want access to more information, and they want to decide what information they'll receive. The Intranet provides Xerox with the ability to offer this "pull" model.

2. The Intranet actually empowers employees. "We've been talking about empowerment for a decade," explains Cahalan, "but we can't empower people without providing the information they need to do their jobs and take initiative."

3. It allows a lot of people in remote sites to work together on their desktops on common efforts, increasing productivity dramatically.

To this can be added the statement that with an Intranet, people are becoming more productive because they now have access to information that heretofore was hidden behind closed doors or in someone's drawer, or in a manual someplace that employees didn't know how to access. Now it's on the Intranet.

An Intranet allows access. It reduces the layers of bureaucracy between an employee's need to know and accessing that information. It allows employees to change their benefits packages and to conduct their own self-paced training. At Sun Microsystems, for example, the Web browser Netscape is serving as a means of searching through CD-ROM training materials, as well as allowing access to sales training information via the Intranet (even though there are bandwidth limits to the Internet currently, it is probable that within a few years greater bandwidth and shorter download times will allow much fuller use of the Internet directly as a training medium).

US West Communication, based in Denver, Colorado, is a telecommunication provider with 50,000 employees in a 14-state region. Its internal Web site includes "The News Stand," a section for late-breaking news; 40 or more internal publications (including graphics and photos) and product catalogs; "The Big Picture," a section coveting the company's mission statements for its different divisions; "This Just In" . . . which includes company and national/international headlines of the day; and "Let's Talk," an interactive forum for employees to discuss issues (Miller, R., 1995).

The Office Away from the Office

One of the major impacts of electronic technologies is that they have empowered executives, managers, and employees to do work without having to congregate in a single location. Of course, we are referring to "knowledge" work, as opposed to manufacturing work. It is obviously difficult to make steel or manufacture a car in different locations (unless, of course, the car is assembled from parts made in disparate locations, but the assembly needs to take place in one location). Electronic technologies, such as laptop computers, mobile phones, telecommunications, e-mail, and the Internet, enable organizational employees to perform work in an office, wherever that might be—in a physical corporate building; in a car, train, bus, plane, ship; at home; or at a restaurant. Electronic technologies allow an employee (manager, or salesperson) to transcend a physical location and function without the benefit of a fixed desk, chair, window, or corner office.

The so-called nontraditional office is no fad or trend. According to *The Wall Street Journal* ". . . at the start of this decade, approximately 9.2 million Americans were working at least part of the week at home . . ." (Sanders, 1994, p. 45). Sanders also reported, "As the workplace becomes more flexible, workers will also be more mobile within the office. Many observers . . . believe that a hallmark of the 21st century workplace will be on the 'nonterritorial' concept, where employees store personal belongings in movable carts, and move from workstation to workstation throughout the day" (p. 45). Sanders continues, "This environment will be particularly appropriate for businesses where people spend only a portion of their time in what are now considered offices. Salespeople, for example, will return to base and use a vacant workstation. The information they need will be stored in computerized databases that they'll access from any workstation or telephone" (p. 45).

Sanders points to several technological developments that will help evolve the "mobile" office:

Today's mouse and keyboard will give way to a digitizing pad on which data are input via pen, finger, or scanner.

Copiers will take on new tasks, such as faxing and translation.

Personal computers (PCs) will routinely have sound and video capabilities, so you can prepare a document while simultaneously watching CNN.

Optical character recognition software, which allows a computer to read text out loud, will greatly improve accuracy on spreadsheets and financial reports.

Voice-text annotation will allow a reader to insert comments on a report by recording them within a document, instead of printing out a hard copy and jotting a note in the margin.

Presentations and reports will be delivered on floppy disks rather than in hard copy printouts. The recipient will review the report, complete with elaborate color graphs, charts, and photographs on their desktop or laptop PCs.

The bulky, boxlike cathode ray tube (CRT) will eventually be replaced by a flat screen than can be popped up or down, as needed, saving space and increasing mobility.

(Sanders, 1994, p. 46)

Chapter 8

Lessons from the Leaders

In this chapter we outline three communications scenarios developed through one-on-one conversations with corporate communication and human resource executives from three major U.S. corporations. Our interviews focused on learning about the evolving nature of internal corporate communications within the targeted companies, through the lens of managing change. In each of the interviews, we asked company representatives to discuss an illustrative communication strategy deployed by the company and the organizational impact thereof within the context of a major change that had been experienced in the last 6 to 12 months.

While some communication studies, such as that of Young and Post (1993), focused on the development of "best practices" criteria, our investigation focused on gleaning detailed snapshots of the organizational impact of employing various communication strategies. Our investigation was not meant to replicate the rigorous design of more scientific studies, but rather to lend insight into how organizations are currently managing the multiple, and sometimes paradoxical, challenges of communication amidst change.

Forms of Change: A Framework for the Lessons

The forms of change being experienced by the three companies we interviewed paralleled those outlined by Kanter and her associates as part of The "Big Three" Model of Change (Kanter, Stein, and Jick, 1992). According to the model, the three forms of change are identity changes, coordination changes, and changes in control. Identity changes focus on the relationships between the organization as an entity and its environment—the assets it

105

owns, the niche it occupies, the relationships it has with its customers, and the like. These changes are related to macroevolutionary forces and to the organization's own capacity to endure over time as a factor in that environment. The Motorola Semi-conductor case reflects this type of change.

Coordination changes involve the internal array of activity sets that constitute the organization. These types of changes are generally related to microevolutionary dynamics of the problems of shape and structure that emerge as organizations grow and age. The ABC Corporation case reflects this type of change. The third form of change, changes in control, relate to political dimensions of organizational activity as they relate to the predominate interest sets, usually who owns or governs the organization. Such changes deal with various levels of "revolution" and are often dramatic in their impact on many aspects of the organization. This type of change is reflected in The Honeywell International case.

While the form of change, and certainly the response to the challenge of change, varied per company, one common thread ran throughout all of the conversations: Certain communication practices, whether formal or informal, greatly bolstered the organization's ability to ride its particular wave of change. The companies we spoke to were not only aware of the power of communication combined with technology but also of the challenge before them in harnessing the power to yield true effectiveness, whether that be the communication of a shared vision or customer service excellence. As one vice president of human resources stated, his greatest learning from employing a new communication strategy was the following: "Be careful not to get caught up in the elegance of what you are doing. You've got a customer who needs to see value and that, in the end, is what counts."

Motorola Semi-Conductor Sector: Communicating Amidst Changes in Identity

To gain a clearer understanding of communication strategies during changes in identity at the Motorola Semi-Conductor Sector, we spoke with Richard (Dick) E. Wintermantel, Vice President and Director of Organization and Leadership Effectiveness. His team's mission is to help operating managers build the global organizational capabilities necessary to achieve business success. To this end, the human resources function had to be reinvented to lead change, become a strategic business partner, and transform the way the human resource professional worked with his or her internal customers.

The Change

The semi-conductor business is an $9 billion part of Motorola. A significant part of the business is non-U.S., with the organization being characterized as very high tech and fast moving, in a state of rapid change. The most significant change to impact the Semi-Conductor Sector came to a head in 1986, when the business was essentially heading "out of business." Competition from Japanese counterparts was fierce, and Motorola was losing market share dramatically. One of the root causes of the challenge to its existence was denial that the business had been severely threatened by this competition.

This macroevolutionary change epitomizes identity change, as it focused on the relationships between Motorola and its environment, specifically with the niche it had become comfortable with "owning" until the pressures of Japanese competition were factored in. This change challenged the organization to examine its capacity to endure over time as a factor in an increasingly competitive environment.

The Change Communication Tools

Dick has developed three simple models for understanding, managing, and communicating change initiatives effectively. Used together, they provide an integrated road map for managers responsible for clearly communicating change. They are:

1. The Agenda Model
2. The Organizational Capabilities Model
3. The FCC Model

The Agenda Model lays out, in three columns going from left to right, guiding parameters (mission, objectives, and vision), strategies and competencies, and action plans. The first guiding parameter, mission, is a simplified statement (seventeen or fewer words) that highlights dimensions of unique value-addedness and customer focus. The second guiding parameter describes the objectives of fulfilling that mission. The third parameter, vision, is characterized as being inspiring, capturing a higher purpose, and focusing on meaningful work for employees and resultant increased commitment by employees. The center column delineates the pivotal strategies developed in response to the change.

These strategies take into account the core competencies of Motorola that will enable the organization to achieve its objectives, fulfill its mission, and realize its vision. The right-hand column outlines, simply, "Who's going to do what, when?" This action piece not only defines next steps but also includes the critical element of accountability for execution. Once the agenda has been created, an easily read one-page poster is created that displays the information in the form as described. These posters are distributed to managers for guidance as they make their way through change initiates. Finally, it should be noted that the Agenda Model requires active participation of the company's leaders, as it is the leader's role to fabricate the agenda.

The Organizational Capabilities Model fundamentally focuses on the plan of the work to be accomplished through the utilization of internal capabilities. The model is short and precise, and focuses on the organizational capabilities and, to some extent, the increasingly virtual structure of the organization. This model is based on the assumption that the success of an organization is not a result of any one factor. As such, two core sets of capabilities are examined—competitive staffing (including intellectual capital, central knowledge and skills, and preferred work styles) and competitive systems (including communication, reward and performance management, business information, financial systems). The staffing and systems capabilities are then designed to be aligned in order to enable the company to execute the pivotal strategies, as outlined through the Agenda.

The FCC Model, a Fundamental Change Communication Model, is based on the following equation:

$$\text{Focus} \times \text{capability} \times \text{commitment} = \text{right results (productivity)}$$

By integrating the dimensions of the first two models (where Focus is represented by the Agenda items, and Capabilities and Commitment are represented in the Organizational Capabilities Model), the FCC Model provides a quick litmus test that determines whether all of the relevant dimensions were explored. Like any other mathematical equation, if one or more elements are missing, the equation is not balanced and thus is rendered meaningless. For example, if Capabilities and Commitment within the context of a change initiative are delineated, but Focus is not, you end up with lots of results, which are not necessarily "right" because they are not aligned.

While the use of these models within the semi-conductor area is prevalent, Motorola encourages, but does not require, other areas to follow suit. Motorola's culture is emerging as an empowered culture, with decreasing reliance on strict policies and procedures. This is not to say that leaders don't provide guidance; they do, in the form of establishing focus for the organization. As Wintermantel comments, " . . . empowerment without focus results in chaos."

No matter which process or combination of processes are used, the desired outputs of any change and strategy focused meetings should be:

1. Definition of the *reason* for the change.
2. Definition of the *focus* of the change.
3. Definition of the *capabilities* to communicate the change.
4. Defined ways to do it *simply*.
5. Defined ways to *internalize* it into the business areas.

The Change Communication Campaign

In response to the identity change being experienced by the company, Motorola developed a two-phase strategy to explore and respond to the issues presented by the mounting competition concerns. The first phase involved "1.1 Day" facilitated meetings, and the second phase involved leveraging the traditional annual executive conference.

The first of what has become annual "1.1 Day" meetings was facilitated by Wintermantel and attended by approximately eighteen global executives who flew in from around the world to take on the challenges presented by this identity change. The meeting was focused, face-to-face, and "low tech," in that they relied on flipcharting for communicating and documenting their discussion. According to Wintermantel, his intent was to help the newly appointed top executives move their leadership team from a transactional approach, traditionally used by managers, to a transformational approach, which is one of the hallmarks of effective-change leaders and leadership teams. Before reaching a level where focus and productivity could occur, the group had to break through the prevalent denial that *there indeed was* a critical problem to focus on. A clinical psychologist was used during this phase as the group learned about its own behavior through application of a technique based on Kubler-Ross' stages of grief. With the denial breakthrough occurring on the first evening, the one-day work session became highly energized, focused, and productive.

A face-to-face conference of Motorola's 500 executives followed, and first focused on the definition of the problem (as arrived upon in the facilitated meetings) and then the rollout of the company's response in the form of an agenda. The eighteen people who were personally involved in creating the agenda in the earlier facilitated meetings took on the responsibility of bringing it back to their respective areas. By exploring their distinctive competencies, Motorola set delineated pivotal strategies, focusing on penetration of the emerging non-U.S. markets and implementation of cultural, systems, and staffing changes aligned to support this strategy to help turnaround the company with regard to its competitive stance.

The Impact

Motorola experienced results within one year of this intervention, and its competitive position has strengthened every consecutive year since 1986. Significant changes in culture, systems, and staffing also occurred as a result of the pivotal strategies first delineated ten years earlier. To this end, Motorola was named one of the top ten most admired companies in a survey conducted by Fortune Magazine (Fisher, 1996). The key attributes assessed for ranking included quality of management, financial soundness, quality of products or services, and the ability to attract, develop, and keep talented people. It would seem unlikely for Motorola to be named in this top ten list today if the change initiative just described did not have a powerful, positive impact.

Lessons Learned

Two lessons emerged as a result of this communication initiate. The first lesson focused on the importance of the power and interplay of the FCC

Model's dimensions. In other words, if either Focus, Commitment, or requisite Capabilities was misunderstood or miscommunicated by management, both the communication and the rollout of the pivotal strategy change initiative would have been rendered ineffective. The interplay of these model dimensions was particularly salient when defining the pivotal strategies.

Another lesson that became clear during the facilitated meetings was that there is a strong connection between how humans and organizations behave when facing a crisis. The prevalence of *denial* became quite clear in the early phases of the initiative and could have debilitated the company further if it was not properly dealt with. The company learned that it had to break through that denial before progress could be made toward their intended goals.

Conclusion

When asked what one development in communication effectiveness he would like to see in the next five years, Wintermantel responded with a goal shared by many organizations during this time of great technology promise, that is, the creation and implementation of the kind of real-time information network that permits individuals to interact in a virtual way. Essentially, an Internet for Motorolans.

ABC Corporation: Communicating Amidst Changes in Coordination

To gain an understanding of the communication of coordination changes at ABC Corporation, a U.S.-based international materials science company, we spoke with the company's former Vice President of Human Resources. His main role for the past four years at the company had been the integration of the human resource function into the overall business system and to develop a positioning process for human resources. Previous to his arrival, the company did not possess a worldwide human resource function, thus this challenging role resembled that of a start-up venture when the project began to take shape two years prior. His reliance on effective internal communication was paramount to the success of this undertaking.

The Change

The most significant change being realized throughout ABC Corporation was the imperative that all of the business units take on strategic responsibility for helping the company become more profitable and grow through innovation. Growth through product innovation was the foundational strength with which the company responded to this strategic imperative. The transformation process occurring within the human resource function was thus driven by the company's recommitment to strategic planning on the part of its business units. This overarching business strategy provided the contextual framework within which the human resource support strategy could be devised and carried out.

Changes in coordination were the basis for the transformation occurring throughout the organization. In taking on the strategic responsibility of growth through innovation, the business units had to re-establish the internal array of activity sets to support the distribution of this responsibility. These microevolutionary organizational changes speak to the problems of shape and structure that emerge as organizations grow and age.

The corporate human resource function, which had previously been done through the work of the CEO and the president, needed to reposition and reinvent itself in order to make a significant impact on the company as a strategic partner. The force for this change was not driven by cost reduction or by complaints from managers, but rather by the need to be strategically aligned to the point that all of the services provided were supporting profitability and innovation. The business challenge presented to the human resource unit was to take advantage of the strengths that currently existed within the company and to globally network the function so that it could be leveraged corporate-wide. The human resource unit was specifically interested in contributing to the organizational change efforts that were occurring system-wide as a result of the business-unit strategic planning initiative.

The Communication Campaign

The communication challenge intrinsic to this repositioning was to define internally how the human resource function could add value to the organization, and thus make a significant impact as a strategic partner. This would require communication strategies that changed the manner in which human resources was perceived and used through the sharing of information, which modeled for the internal audience the role they were taking on. The main dimensions of the communication were focused on marketing how the human resource function would:

1. Support the defined strategy through the activities it undertook
2. Function as a backup for the business units in their change efforts to align with the stated strategy
3. Provide critical employee communication to strategic divisions
4. Design a human resource organization that responded to the strategy

To respond to this challenge, ABC Corporation employed a communication change model that emphasized consistency and richness. For consistency, a common communication package was created for all human resource professionals to ensure there was no variance in the message to be communicated. In terms of richness, the first media venue employed was the richest possible, face to face. The change initiative required the human resource function to essentially make a sale to the business units and communicate the personal intent to become more strategically aligned.

Through business team presentations and regional visits, the human resource unit communicated its strategy to its internal audience, without whom the strategy would not be effective. These communication activities focused on gleaning input on the translation of business needs into the human resource function response to those needs. The strongest data gathered through this process was perception data; it was critical for the human resources unit to understand how other units defined the human resource role within the larger organization.

A companion media employed was written communication, in the form of a two-phase survey process. In the first phase, human resources gathered data on the current culture within which human resources operated. The information was then fed back to the constituents to gain clarification around the data's meaning, in the context of human resource service to the larger organization. Two years later, the company was resurveyed to determine:

1. How human resources was performing in the eyes of the business units they served
2. What priorities were held by the business units, in terms of the services required from human resources
3. The existence of gaps in service, perception, or responsiveness
4. If the needs of the business units had changed since the first survey

The timing of this communication initiative was "all at once." In order to impart the importance and urgency of the repositioning, the human resource unit chose a strategy that quickly infused the organization with its new direction and produced a strong impact.

Organization Design

The organization design of the human resource unit was quite purposeful in that it needed to support the new role of human resources and sustain it throughout the changing environment. ABC Corporation employed benchmarking teams to determine what other companies were doing to relate human resource strategy to corporate strategy and to establish linkages between human resources and the business units. Basic design criteria were established and in September 1993, the company began staffing the new human resource organization, using as many existing employees as possible. Some people were added from outside sources, some chose to leave the organization, and still others were recruited from line positions. A decentralized approach was taken by creating a division human resource director for each line of business, in partnership with line managers. This enhanced the probability that the communication between human resources and the business units would be targeted, relevant, and supportive of the change they were undertaking. A small corporate human resource group was also organized around three key areas: change management, leadership development, and rewards and recognition. A worldwide human resources council comprised of human resource leaders from geography, business, and corporate realms was established as a key linkage. With this structure, the human resource function was able to work across more fluid communication boundaries and to enable the human resource professionals in divisional positions to speak the language of the internal customers they served.

The Impact

The former Vice President of Human Resources characterized this change effort as meeting with mixed success. What was being taken on by the human resource organization was very new to this company, and change does not occur overnight. Certainly, though, the impact was felt throughout the organization on a few important dimensions.

Human Resource Function Identity. The organization was quite successful in instilling pride within the human resource function, adopting the logo of a compass to be a metaphor for their role in helping guide the change efforts of other business units. Existing challenges remain because other business units are still getting used to human resources as an integrated service within the larger context. Furthermore, while the impact of this change is not quantifiable, as are cost-cutting imperatives, the benchmarking for success is adding value, although difficult to measure.

Increased Participation. A positive impact resulting from the second round of surveys was a dramatic increase in the level of *participation*, as depicted by the survey response rates. This level signaled an increase in commitment to the change efforts occurring throughout the system and the role the human resource function was playing in support of them. Overall, a much higher level of disclosure was practiced by line professionals throughout the organization around strategically important human resource issues.

New Language. In addition, the communication had effectively equipped line managers to discuss human resource issues in more integrative, and thus more meaningful, ways. The communication campaign had effectively instilled a new vocabulary with which line managers were conducting business, with inherent focus on retention of key talent, employee career resilience, professional development, incorporation of feedback techniques, and increased awareness of the characteristics of effective leaders. Through the development of a common language platform, the human resource initiative was also lending strength to the overall effectiveness of ABC Corporation's internal communication practices.

New Learning.   The repositioning efforts had effectively set the stage for continual communication to the business units focusing on the learning from the strategic planning imperative delineated by senior management. On a quarterly basis, the human resource unit now communicates a progress report on:

- Organizational change efforts
- Quality management reviews
- Rewards
- Specific examples of internal organizational change activities to date

Conclusion

Like other organizations, ABC Corporation is challenged with the demands of globalization. While they have been successful at employing high-touch, rather than high-tech communication strategies to date, the challenges of being geographically dispersed are formidable. Dealing with crossing time zones and heavy travel has certainly impacted their change efforts. Furthermore, it should also be noted that the previous CEO was a strong ally in the repositioning of human resources. With the recent introduction of a new CEO, only time will tell as a more powerful form of change, that of control, is ushered in. But as the vice president's quote articulated earlier, it is not the elegance of your activities that matters, but rather whether you have delivered value. It would seem at this juncture in their change efforts that the organization's human resource organization has done just that.

Honeywell: Communicating Amidst Changes in Control

To better understand the communication activities amidst changes in control, we spoke with Sue Plaster, Director of Employee Communication Worldwide, at Honeywell, Inc. In addition to the interview content, Sue shared with us a speech she gave at The Conference Board West Coast Corporate Communications Conference in September 1995. In her role, she is responsible for employee communication for 50,000 employees within Honeywell. Her main objective in her communication is the delivery of communication regarding news, vision, strategy, and values, with the ultimate goal of "building momentum" toward strategic change goals.

The Change

The most significant change being experienced by Honeywell is a realignment around a common vision and strategy as championed by its new CEO. Historically, communication on company purpose, vision, and strategy had been delivered in the traditional top-down manner. The employee communications professionals, with the guidance of the new CEO's communication priorities, had to redesign the way in which change communication was delivered, and thus interpreted, within the organization. According to Kanter et al.'s Big Three Model of Change, the change being experienced by Honeywell is the most dramatic form of change in terms of its impact on the organization. Changes in control, as in the case of the new CEO ushering in a completely new communication culture, relates to political dimensions of organizational activity because they relate to which interests or interest sets predominate. Such changes deal with various levels of "revolution," which is reflected in Honeywell's transformational impacts and learning.

From a business perspective, Honeywell experienced a decade, from 1982 to 1992, best characterized as static. Significant growth did not occur during this time, nor was growth delineated as a strategic priority. In 1993, with the introduction of the new CEO, Michael Bonsignore, a dramatic growth strategy was put into place, with the goal of growing from a $6 billion dollar company to a $10 billion company by the year 2000. All of the major change occurring in the company since the introduction of this initiative has been driven by the company's pursuit of growth. Plaster likens this cultural change to the videogame "Mortal Kombat," as a percentage of companies will not survive unless they undergo significant change.

In order to garner support for this growth initiative, senior management at Honeywell felt a strong need to develop a common vision and values. What was of paramount importance to management was the *content* of the communication, its ultimate message, which precipitated speed of delivery and/or acceptance of the message. The growth strategy was designed around a three-part vision, comprised of three "whats," or those business growth parameters on which the strategy focused and five "hows," or the five vehicles through which growth in these areas would be accomplished. The three "whats" are (1) financial performance, (2) customer delight, and (3) leadership in control (industry and market related). The five vehicles for achieving growth in the three delineated areas are (1) people, (2) integrity, (3) quality, (4) technology, and (5) global presence.

The Change Communication Campaign

The media selected for this communication campaign had to be altered to fit the message. In order to effectively bring employees to an enhanced level of awareness and acceptance of the values and vision, Honeywell determined that the chosen media had to possess the three following characteristics:

1. It had to be rapid; thus, *speed* was paramount.
2. It had to be two way; thus, allowing for *dialogue.*
3. It had to be personal and conversational, thus setting the stage for *openness.*

Two-way dialogue was somewhat of a departure from the previous character of the company. The focus on speed, dialogue, and openness helped galvanize a common platform for the new design of internal communication within the company. Although communication on such paramount issues as vision and values must originate at the top, a top-down character was avoided by communicating in an open-ended manner, inviting responses from employees. The company values were created after holding numerous focus groups and sensing sessions, which was not in any way a top-down process.

In order to ensure that communications were both received and understood, Honeywell employed multiple two-way media for sending its messages. For example, during his first three months in office, CEO Bonsignore sent company vision messages directly from his office to employees through a variety of media. Employees received voice-mails, e-mails, and face-to-face and video communications from the CEO. The video communication was coupled with feedback cards to allow employees to feedback responses and ideas pertaining to the CEO's message and to ensure two-way communication. His goal was to have each employee hear the vision from him ten times.

In terms of timing, major communications and announcements of greater importance were delivered both "all at once" through a variety of media and continuously to reinforce understanding and commitment. Another communication dynamic that was given renewed priority by Honeywell's new CEO was *consistency*. This consistency was achieved through (1) repeated exposure of the CEO to employees, (2) the employment of a variety of media to respond to various learning styles, and (3) targeted written communication for specific locations, highlighting the message in light of their particular issues.

The redesigned communication platform focused on both the repositioning of vision and values, and also on the more targeted and day-to-day operations. The company publishes an electronic newsletter, *Honeywell Headlines*, which reaches more than 30,000 people on e-mail and tracks the progress toward the company vision one week at a time. There is also a daily broadcast news service, called "Honeywell Headline News," which averages 3,000 listeners per month. Employees can phone in for the company's daily three-minute news broadcast, along with a current stock quote. Special electronic bulletins are also sent out worldwide when there is breaking news, reaching employees before the external news media does. These uses of electronic media demonstrate an increased reliance on technology to enhance effective communication. Three years ago, according to Plaster, less than 10 percent of Honeywell's employee communications were electronic. Today, it's 40 percent, with the print-to-electronic ratio expected to even out within the next three years. Some examples of the application of the new communication techniques follow.

Video.   All employee videos are first pretested with employee focus groups, which are considered partner/owners to the communication process. The feedback gleaned from these groups helps gauge the audience's understanding of the messages. Honeywell also previews videos via video-conferencing outside the United States to ensure that the communication is globally accepted and not ethnocentric.

Once the videos have been designed to specification, they are distributed company-wide. For each all-employee video distributed throughout the system, an average of 1,200 employees return feedback cards. Locations are given video facilitation guides and are later polled to determine employee reactions to the video and to collect data such as where and when the video was shown.

Voice-Mail. In addition to company-wide e-mail, another medium used at Honeywell is voice-mail, particularly an all-employee voice-mail. This technique uses a two- to three-minute broadcasting message from the CEO and can be targeted to groups ranging in size from 5 to 20,000. Often this technique is used to congratulate recipients of quality awards or other such unit distinctions or accomplishments. Like all other communication vehicles, the all-employee voice-mails were two way, allowing employees to respond to the message. Furthermore, voice-mails can be targeted to employees at specific employee locations. For example, Bonsignore might send a message only to employees at a location he just visited or a location that has just won an award.

Screen Savers. In order for employees to remember to apply the company's new vision statement, a company screen saver was created for all employees' computers.

Overall, both media and message dominate at Honeywell. As the communication is characterized as rapid, responsive, responsible, two way, and exploratory, employees have an impact on the communication directed at them. There is an intrinsic responsibility that has been built into communication activities at the company, and employees take on the responsibility of reading, understanding, and acting on the communications they receive. Inasmuch as the communication has been tailored to its audience, its audience responds in kind and becomes active players in what has become a very dynamic communication environment. Again, this new environment is a dramatic departure from that which prevailed under the former CEO.

A few comments are in order on the costs associated with becoming technology dependent for communication. While there are certainly substantial costs in the original investment, the return on technology investment can be substantial. For example, thanks to e-mail, the departmental phone bill within the communications unit is now one quarter of what it was eighteen months before. This equates to a saving of tens of thousands of dollars. In fact, e-mail has become so critical to workflow at Honeywell that when the communications department takes on a major new vendor it is imperative that electronic links are set up between them from day one. "Whether it is action reports from meetings, proposals, or daily correspondence, we expect to get them on e-mail." (Interestingly, Plaster reports that not even half of the Fortune 200 companies are currently using technology to get feedback about employee communications.) Another example of cost savings is the *Honeywell Headlines* weekly newsletter mentioned earlier. This electronic bulletin replaced a monthly print newsletter that cost the company $150,000 annually.

The other costs of technology are, of course, the time and incredible effort that needs to be invested in getting responsive systems up and running. Plaster notes there are still obstacles to overcome at Honeywell, and the development of the architecture of the system dealt with the dark side of technology, including panic when their file server first crashed, as this caused the company to lose two years worth of work dedicated to the building of distribution lists.

The Impact

Choices in communication media, content, and timing can impact organizations in a number of important ways. The new communication techniques employed by Honeywell impacted the organization in four ways.

Information Turnaround.   Both the speed with which information was distributed, shared, and responded to and the quantity of usable information greatly increased with the introduction of the new commitment to effective communication. For example, through e-mail publications, employees were able to stay abreast of the top news stories that impacted Honeywell, in both its internal and external environments. Knowledge of this news allowed employees to act in a more information-rich environment that valued disclosure, and they thus were able to make better decisions because the stories helped them get a global perspective.

Cultural Reactivity.   Using faster, more responsive avenues for communicating ideas, inquiries, and problems helped transform the very character of the company's culture from slow and passive to quick, responsive, and probably most importantly, proactive. This proactivity indicated to senior management that employees were becoming involved in the shared sense of responsibility for moving the company ahead. In other words, communication was enabling Honeywell to foster a culture of change.

Openness.   As a result of the CEO's commitment to speed, dialogue, and openness, he has received an increasing number of personal notes from employees, sharing their ideas for shaping and supporting the change initiative brought on by the growth strategy. According to Plaster, five out of ten respondents to the CEO's voice-mails are writing to thank the CEO for his communication, four out of ten offer him information or ask for help, and one of ten delivers a critique. He has also received fewer anonymous communications, which highlights an increased trust on the part of employees, who feel that their messages will be treated with the attention and respect they deserve. This decrease in anonymity also hints towards an increase in employees taking on responsibility for their role in the communication environment.

Organizational Behavior. The new communication environment also fostered an increase in a variety of behaviors that help support the growth strategy. Specifically, increased use of team-based project work and brainstorming techniques were witnessed after the introduction of the shared information venues. Other changes included faster and more prevalent decision making on the part of employees, as well as the recognition of knowledge asset development as key to the accomplishment of the growth goals set before them.

Organization Design

It should be noted that the design of the Honeywell communication organization was quite purposeful. The Directors of Communication within the business unit, regions, and the corporate organization report to the Vice President of Communication, who in turn reports to the CEO. The structure remains centralized so as to benefit from and communicate effectively and consistently the CEO's perspective. This alignment vis-à-vis the CEO's position was seen as critical to the effectiveness of communicating the CEO's message. While the structure of the communication unit was key, the overall company structure became more of a moot issue, as the communication focused on the audience and essentially removed the boundaries imposed by structure through the use of electronic media for what is essentially mass communication.

Lessons Learned

Honeywell began this cultural transformation with one major underlying belief: The more information that can be put in employees' hands in a responsible way, the more likely they will be to effect change because they will understand the impact of it. Some lessons that emerged as a result of carrying this belief through the deployment of the new communication strategy follow.

1. *Planned involvement.* Honeywell realized great strides in communication effectiveness by simply involving employees beforehand. By educating people on what's coming, they are prepared not only for the content of the communication but are also in a better position to understand its implications and thus to act on it. The use of targeted focus groups and the continued use

of techniques such as feedback cards kept employees involved in the communication process and kept Honeywell's communication professionals in touch with their audience.

2. *Technology use.*   According to Plaster, Honeywell is communicating in ways it wouldn't have dreamed of five years ago. Because Honeywell is a global company with global customers, it must have the electronic infrastructure to support fast, effective, and global communications. For example, the company's communications group no longer retypes news stories sent to them from communicators across the world and they e-mail stories worldwide for review. They transfer copy in other languages for use in speeches and brochures. And they provide informative issue backgrounders on demand through an electronic forwarding service on e-mail.

3. *Measurement.*   Collecting data before and after communicating has become a priority at Honeywell. Although information gleaned from focus groups isn't as quantitative as surveys, Honeywell communications feels the data quality received is a good tradeoff. For example, they use focus groups to test new communications pieces before printing as a way to tailor the message and medium to the audience receiving them. In developing its 1995 communications plan, the communications group talked with more than 100 employees via teleconference, videoconferences, e-mail, and in person. Although significant time was spent getting feedback and analyzing it, the plan, when complete, was reality based. Electronic and print surveys also are used to measure the effectiveness of communications.

4. *Training and development.*   With the active involvement of all 50,000 Honeywell employees in the new communication environment, the need for greater focus on training and development was heightened. In order to have its employees effectively participate as responsible communication partners, Honeywell had to examine the developmental implications of this new behavior. Certainly, computer and other technology-based training has been emphasized. This lesson could not be overemphasized, as it is the collective individual employee's communication competencies that determine the overall system's effectiveness.

Conclusion

The continual changes being experienced at Honeywell are company-wide and focus on where the company is going and where it will ultimately be in the context of a rapidly changing business environment. The consistent translation of this message to the employees is paramount in importance to its senior management. Evolving the content of communication to a higher level, to impart true understanding to its audience, has allowed Honeywell to educate its employees on its "change priorities," amidst rapid growth and ever-changing conditions. And this, ultimately, is what effective communication can accomplish for a change-infused environment—the ability to synergize employee actions toward prioritized issues, so that the company can work together to make real progress on its stated goals.

Plaster quoted a phenomenon articulated by Jack Welch in her speech: "The people who know about the problem won't or can't or are afraid to get the message to the boss." It seems that Honeywell is making a concerted effort to eradicate this problem through the speed, dialogue, and openness characteristic of its new communication environment.

Chapter 9

The Seven New Rules of Corporate Communication

Given the challenges organizations will be facing in the next millennium, the following will be the new rules of corporate discourse in the landscape of organizations of the future:

1. *Effective communication behaviors, processes, and systems must be considered as strategic imperatives.* CEOs must take on the responsibility of designing, directing, supporting, and valuing communication sophistication within their organizations. The organizations that reach higher levels of communication sophistication will be competitively superior and a magnet for first-class workers.

2. *Effective communication is everyone's responsibility and will become a highly critical performance criteria.* Every player in the new corporate landscape—executive, manager, core member, contingent worker, alliance partner—is a communication manager, with the requisite roles and responsibilities.

3. *Effective communication requires continual learning and development.* Every player in the new corporate landscape will be challenged to continually enhance his or her communication savvy, whether that be in the area of climatic, technical, or behavioral expertise. Furthermore, organizations must "learn how to learn" in order to enhance their communication efficacy and thus their competitiveness.

4. *Diversity both challenges and enriches communication practices.* Cognitive diversity is the new diversity benchmark and will contribute significantly to an organization's relative communication sophistication. Organizations must pass the racial, gender, and cultural diversity threshold in order to enter an environment where cognitive diversity is valued.

5. *Network organizations provide the most efficacious communication environment.*   Organizations should be "correctly bounded" to allow for a flow of communication appropriate for its environment and culture. The emerging network organization structure will require attention to the critical issues of boundaries, relationships, and networking expertise.

6. *Organizational cultures exert a powerful impact on the effectiveness of communication behaviors, processes, and systems.*   Organizational culture will increasingly determine a company's ability to harness the power of effective communication, that is, to create understanding and make knowledge more productive. As these cultures change and evolve in response to climatic shifts, so must the organization.

7. *Continual networking will be the preferred mode for highly effective communicators.*   Networking communication competencies will be the most highly valued skills in the organization of the future. These competencies are a prerequisite to designing and sustaining the network organizations of the future.

Appendix I

The Emerging Employment Landscape

Electronic media have not only had an impact on the shape of American corporations and the relationship between managers and employees, they have also had a major influence on the number and kinds of work available to current and future generations of workers. In the year ending June 1995, according to an American Management Association (AMA) survey, 50 percent of the large and midsize companies eliminated jobs; the percentage has risen each year since 1991. Most also created jobs—hiring with one hand, firing with the other. Net, their labor forces shrank just 1.1 percent, with other companies picking up the slack. Among the 1,003 companies surveyed, total employment rose 4.5 percent. The losers? Middle management. The winners? Professional and technical jobs, which are being created 50 percent faster than they are being cut (Stewart, 1996).

Every two years, the Bureau of Labor Statistics develops projections of the labor force, economic growth, industry output and employment, and occupational employment under three sets of alternative assumptions, low, moderate, and high. These projections cover a 10- to 15-year period and provide a framework for the discussion of job outlook in each occupational statement in its *Handbook*. This appendix uses the moderate alternative of each projection to provide a framework for individual job-outlook discussions.

Population Trends

Employment opportunities are affected by population trends in several ways. Changes in the size and composition of the population between 1992 and 2005 will influence the demand for goods and services. For example, the population aged 85 and over will grow about four times as fast as the total population, increasing the demand for health services. Population changes also produce corresponding changes in the size and characteristics of the labor force.

Geographic Shifts

Population growth varies greatly among geographic regions, affecting the demand for goods and services and, in turn, workers in various occupations and industries. Between 1979 and 1992, the population of the Midwest and the Northeast grew by only 3 percent and 4 percent, respectively, compared with 19 percent in the South and 30 percent in the West. These differences reflect the movement of people seeking new jobs or retiring, as well as higher birth rates in some areas than in others.

Projections by the Bureau of the Census indicate that the West and South will continue to be the fastest growing regions, increasing 24 percent and 16 percent, respectively, between 1992 and 2005. The Midwest population is expected to grow by 7 percent, while the number of people in the Northeast is projected to increase by only 3 percent. Geographic shifts in the population alter the demand for and the supply of workers in local job markets. Moreover, in areas dominated by one or two industries, local job markets may be extremely sensitive to the economic conditions of those industries.

Growth Occupations

Three out of the four fastest growing occupational groups will be executive, administrative, and managerial; professional specialty; and technicians and related support occupations. These occupations generally require the highest levels of education and skill, and will make up an increasing proportion of new jobs. Office and factory automation, changes in consumer demand, and movement of production facilities to offshore locations are expected to cause employment to stagnate or decline in many occupations that require little formal education, for example, apparel workers and textile machinery operators. Opportunities for those who do not finish high school will be increasingly limited, and workers who are not literate may not even be considered for most jobs.

Those who do not complete high school and are employed are more likely to have low-paying jobs with little advancement potential, while workers in occupations requiring higher levels of education have higher incomes. In addition, many of the occupations projected to grow most rapidly between 1992 and 2005 are among those with higher earnings. Nevertheless, even slower growing occupations that have a large number of workers will provide many job openings because the need to replace workers who leave the labor force or transfer to other occupations accounts for most job openings. Consequently, workers with all levels of education and training will continue to be in demand, although advancement opportunities generally will be best for those with the most education and training.

In recent years, the level of educational attainment of the labor force has risen dramatically. In 1992, 27 percent of all workers aged 25 and over had a bachelor's degree or higher, while only 12 percent did not possess a high school diploma. The trend toward higher educational attainment is expected to continue. Projected rates of employment growth are faster for occupations requiring higher levels of education or training than for those requiring less.

Employment Change

Total employment is expected to increase from 121.1 million in 1992 to 147.5 million in 2005, or by 22 percent. The 26.4 million jobs that will be added to the U.S. economy by 2005 will not be evenly distributed across major industrial and occupational groups, causing some restructuring of employment. Continued faster than average employment growth among occupations that require relatively high levels of education or training is expected.

Industry Profile

The long-term shift from goods-producing to service-producing employment is expected to continue. For example, service-producing industries, including transportation, communications, and utilities; retail and wholesale trade; services; government; and finance, insurance, and real estate, are expected to account for approximately 24.5 million of the 26.4 million job growth over the 1992 to 2005 period. In addition, the services division within this sector, which includes health, business, and educational services, contains 15 of the 20 fastest growing industries. Expansion of service-sector employment is linked to a number of factors, including changes in consumer tastes and preferences, legal and regulatory changes, advances in science and technology, and changes in the way businesses are organized and managed. Specific factors responsible for varying growth prospects in major industry divisions are discussed later.

Service-Producing Industries

Services is both the largest and the fastest growing division within the service-producing sector. This division provided 38.6 million jobs in 1992;

employment is expected to rise 40 percent to 54.2 million by 2005, accounting for almost two thirds of all new jobs. Jobs will be found in small firms and in large corporations, and in industries as diverse as hospitals, data processing, and management consulting. Health services and business services are projected to continue to grow very quickly. In addition, social, legal, and engineering and management services industry growth further illustrate this division's strong growth.

Health services will continue to be one of the fastest growing industries in the economy, with employment increasing from 9.6 to 13.8 million. Improvements in medical technology and a growing and aging population will increase the demand for health services. Employment in home healthcare services, the second fastest growing industry in the economy, nursing homes, and offices and clinics of physicians and other health practitioners is projected to increase rapidly. However, not all health industries will grow at the same rate. Despite being the largest healthcare industry, hospitals will grow more slowly than most other health services industries.

Business services industries also will generate many jobs. Employment is expected to grow from 5.3 million in 1992 to 8.3 million in 2005. Personnel supply services, made up primarily of temporary help agencies, is the largest sector in this group and will increase by 57 percent, from 1.6 to 2.6 million jobs. However, due to the slowdown in labor force participation by young women, and the proliferation of personnel supply firms in recent years, this industry will grow more slowly than during the 1979 to 1992 period.

Business services also includes one of the fastest growing industries in the economy, computer and data processing services. This industry's rapid growth stems from advances in technology, worldwide trends toward office and factory automation, and increases in demand from business firms, government agencies, and individuals.

Education is expected to add 2.8 million jobs to the 9.7 million in 1992. This increase reflects population growth and, in turn, rising enrollments projected for elementary, secondary, and postsecondary schools. The elementary school age population (age 5 to 13) will rise by 2.8 million between 1992 and 2005, the secondary school age (age 14 to 17) by 3.4 million, and the traditional postsecondary school age (age 18 to 24) by 2.2 million. In addition, continued rising enrollments of older, foreign, and part-time students are expected to enhance employment in postsecondary education. Not all of the increase in employment in education, however, will be for teachers; teacher aides, counselors, and administrative staff also are projected to increase.

Social services employment is expected to increase by 1.7 million, bringing the total to 3.7 million by 2005, reflecting the growing elderly population. For example, residential care institutions, which provide around-the-clock assistance to older persons and others who have limited ability for self-care, is projected to be the fastest growing industry in the U.S. economy. Other social services industries projected to grow rapidly include child daycare services and individual and miscellaneous social services, which includes elderly daycare and family social services.

Employment in *wholesale and retail trade* is expected to rise by 19 and 23 percent, respectively, from 6 to 7.2 million in wholesale trade and from 19.3 to 23.8 million in retail trade. Spurred by higher levels of personal income, the fastest projected job growth in retail trade is in apparel and accessory stores, and appliance, radio, television, and music stores. Substantial numerical increases in retail employment are anticipated in large industries, including eating and drinking places, food stores, automotive dealerships and service stations, and general merchandise stores.

Finance, insurance, and real estate. Employment is expected to increase by 21 percent, adding 1.4 million jobs to the 1992 level of 6.6 million. The strong demand for financial services is expected to continue. Bank mergers, consolidations, and closings resulting from overexpansion and competition from nonbank corporations that offer banklike services are expected to limit job growth among commercial banks and savings and loan associations. The fastest growing industries within this sector are expected to be holding and investment offices and mortgage bankers and brokers. Insurance agents, brokers, and services is expected to register the largest numerical increase in jobs.

Transportation, communications, and public utilities. Overall employment will increase by 14 percent. Employment in the transportation sector is expected to increase by 24 percent, from 3.5 to 4.3 million jobs. Truck transportation will account for 50 percent of all new jobs; air transportation will account for 29 percent. The projected gains in transportation jobs reflect the continued shift from rail to road freight transportation, rising personal incomes, and growth in foreign trade. In addition, deregulation in the transportation industry has increased personal and business travel options, spurring strong job growth in the passenger transportation arrangement industry, which includes travel agencies. Reflecting labor-saving technology and industry competition, employment in communications is projected to decline by 12 percent. Employment in utilities, however, is expected to grow, adding 117,000 new jobs, highlighted by strong growth in water supply and sanitary services.

Government employment, between 1992 and 2005, excluding public education and public hospitals, is expected to increase 10 percent, from 9.5 million to 10.5 million jobs. Growth will be driven by state and local government. Employment in the federal government and U.S. Postal Service is expected to decline by 113,000 and 41,000 jobs, respectively.

Goods-Producing Industries

Employment in this sector has not recovered from the recessionary period of the early 1980s and the trade imbalances that began in the mid-1980s.

Although overall employment in goods-producing industries is expected to show little change, growth prospects within the sector vary considerably.

Construction employment is expected to increase by 26 percent from 4.5 to 5.6 million. The need to improve the nation's infrastructure, resulting in increases in road, bridge, and tunnel construction, will offset the slowdown in demand for new housing, reflecting the slowdown in population growth and the overexpansion of office building construction in recent years.

Manufacturing employment is expected to decline by 3 percent from the 1992 level of 18 million. The projected loss of manufacturing jobs reflects productivity gains achieved from increased investment in manufacturing technologies. The composition of manufacturing employment is expected to shift because most of the jobs that will disappear are production jobs. On the other hand, the number of professional positions in manufacturing firms will increase.

Occupational Profile

Continued expansion of the service-producing sector conjures up an image of a workforce dominated by cashiers, retail sales workers, and waiters. Although service-sector growth will generate millions of these jobs, it also will create jobs for financial managers, engineers, nurses, electrical and electronics technicians, and many other managerial, professional, and technical workers. As indicated earlier, the fastest growing occupations will be those that require the most formal education and training.

This section furnishes an overview of projected employment in eight categories or clusters of occupations that we felt were most relevant to readers of this book. The clusters are based on the Standard Occupational Classification (SOC) and are used by all federal agencies that collect occupational employment data, and is the organizational framework for grouping statements in the *Handbook*.

1. *Professional specialty occupations.*   Workers in these occupations perform a wide variety of duties and are employed in almost every industry. Employment in this cluster is expected to grow by 37 percent, from 16.6 to 22.8 million jobs, making it the fastest growing occupational cluster in the economy. Human services workers, computer scientists and systems analysts, physical therapists, special education teachers, and operations research analysts are among the fastest growing professional specialty occupations.

2. *Service occupations.*   This group includes a wide range of workers in protective services, food and beverage preparation, health services, and cleaning and personal services. Employment in these occupations is expected to grow by 33 percent, faster than average, from 19.4 to 25.8 million. Service occupations that are expected to experience both fast growth and large job growth

include homemaker–home health aides, nursing aides, childcare workers, guards, and correction officers.

3. *Technicians and related support occupations.* Workers in this group provide technical assistance to engineers, scientists, physicians, and other professional workers, as well as operate and program technical equipment. Employment in this cluster is expected to increase 32 percent, faster than average, from 4.3 to 5.7 million.

Employment of paralegals is expected to increase much faster than average as use of these workers in the rapidly expanding legal services industry increases. Health technicians and technologists, such as licensed practical nurses and radiological technologists, will add large numbers of jobs. Growth in other occupations, such as broadcast technicians, will be limited by laborsaving technological advances.

4. *Executive, administrative, and managerial occupations.* Workers in this cluster establish policies, make plans, determine staffing requirements, and direct the activities of businesses, government agencies, and other organizations. Employment in this cluster is expected to increase by 26 percent, from 12.1 to 15.2 million, reflecting average growth. Growth will be spurred by the increasing number and complexity of business operations and will result in large employment gains, especially in the services industry division. However, many businesses will streamline operations by employing fewer managers, thus offsetting increases in employment.

Like other occupations, changes in managerial and administrative employment reflect industry growth, and utilization of managers and administrators. For example, employment of health services managers will grow much faster than average, while wholesale and retail buyers are expected to grow more slowly than average.

Hiring requirements in many managerial and administrative jobs are becoming more stringent. Work experience, specialized training, or graduate study will be increasingly necessary. Familiarity with computers will continue to be important as a growing number of firms rely on computerized management information systems.

5. *Marketing and sales occupations.* Workers in this cluster sell goods and services, purchase commodities and property for resale, and stimulate consumer interest. Employment in this cluster is projected to increase by 21 percent, from 13 to 15.7 million jobs, about as fast as average. Demand for travel agents is expected to grow much faster than average. Due to strong growth in the industries that employ them, services sales representatives, securities and financial services sales workers, and real estate appraisers will experience faster than average growth. Many part- and full-time job openings are expected for retail sales workers and cashiers due to the large size and high turnover associated with these occupations. Opportunities for higher paying sales jobs, however, will tend to be more competitive.

6. *Mechanics, installers, and repairers.* These workers adjust, maintain, and repair automobiles, industrial equipment, computers, and many other types of equipment. Overall employment in these occupations is expected to grow by 16 percent, from 4.8 to 5.6 million, due to increased use of mechanical and electronic equipment. The fastest growing occupation in this group is expected to be data processing equipment repairers, reflecting the increased use of these types of machines. Communications equipment mechanics, installers, and repairers, and telephone and cable television line installers and repairers, in sharp contrast, are expected to record a decline in employment due to laborsaving advances.

7. *Administrative support occupations, including clerical.* Workers in this largest major occupational group perform a wide variety of administrative tasks necessary to keep organizations functioning smoothly. The group as a whole is expected to grow by 14 percent, from 22.3 to 25.4 million jobs, about as fast as the average. Technological advances are projected to slow employment growth for stenographers, typists, and word processors. Receptionists and information clerks will grow faster than average, spurred by rapidly expanding industries such as business services. Because of their large size and substantial turnover, clerical occupations will offer abundant opportunities for qualified job seekers in the years ahead.

8. *Production occupations.* Workers in these occupations set up, install, adjust, operate, and tend machinery and equipment and use hand tools to fabricate and assemble products. Little change in the 1992 employment level of 12.2 million is expected due to increases in imports, overseas production, and automation. Relative to other occupations, employment in many production occupations is more sensitive to the business cycle and competition from imports.

Replacement Needs

Most jobs through the year 2005 will become available as a result of replacement needs. Replacement openings occur as people leave occupations. Some transfer to other occupations as a step up the career ladder or change careers. Others stop working in order to return to school, assume household responsibilities, or retire. Thus, even occupations with little or no employment growth or slower than average employment growth still may offer many job openings.

The number of replacement openings and the proportion of job openings made up by replacement needs vary by occupation. Occupations with the most replacement openings generally are large, with low pay and status, low training requirements, and a high proportion of young and part-time workers. Occupations with relatively few replacement openings tend to be associated with high pay and status, lengthy training requirements, and a high proportion of prime working age, full-time workers. Workers in these occupations generally acquire education or training that often is not applicable to other occupations. For example, among professional specialty occupations, only 38 percent of total job opportunities result from replacement needs, as opposed to 78 percent among production occupations.

Job Outlooks

The outlook for jobs in various management and staff positions is telling with respect to shifting managerial issues and roles in the changing corporate landscape. The following section examines job outlooks for five key categories of roles that will be played out in the emerging employment landscape.

I. Management Analysts and Consultants

Employment of management analysts and consultants is expected to grow much faster than the average for all occupations through the year 2005 as industry and government increasingly rely on outside expertise to improve the performance of their organizations. Growth is expected in large consulting firms, but also in small consulting firms whose consultants specialize in highly specific areas of expertise. Although most job openings will result from employment growth of the occupation, additional opportunities will arise from the need to replace personnel who transfer to other fields or leave the labor force.

Increased competition has caused American industry to take a closer look at its operations. In more competitive international and domestic markets, firms cannot afford inefficiency and wasted resources or else they risk losing their share of the market. Management consultants are being increasingly relied on to help reduce costs, streamline operations, and develop marketing strategies. As businesses downsize and eliminate functions as well as permanent staff, consultants will be used to perform those functions on a contractual basis. On the other hand, businesses undergoing expansion, particularly into world markets, will also need the skills of management consultants to help with organizational, administrative, and other issues.

Continuing changes in the business environment also are expected to lead to demand for management consultants: Firms will use consultants' expertise to incorporate new technologies, to cope with more numerous and complex government regulations, and to adapt to a changing labor force. As businesses rely more on technology, there are increasing roles for consultants with a technical background, such as engineering or biotechnology, particularly when combined with an MBA.

Federal, state, and local agencies also are expected to expand their use of management analysts. In the era of budget deficits, analysts' skills at identifying problems and implementing cost-reduction measures are expected to become increasingly important. However, because one half of the management analysts employed by the federal government work for the Department of Defense, the pace of federal employment growth will vary with the defense budget. In the private sector, job opportunities are expected to be best for those with a graduate degree and some industry expertise, while opportunities for those with only a bachelor's degree will be best in the federal government.

Despite projected rapid employment growth, competition for jobs as management consultants is expected to be keen in the private sector. Because management consultants can come from such diverse educational backgrounds, the pool of applicants from which employers hire is quite large. Additionally, the independent and challenging nature of the work, combined with high earnings potential, make this occupation attractive to many.

II. General Managers and Top Executives

Employment of general managers and top executives is expected to grow more slowly than the average for all occupations through the year 2005 as companies restructure managerial hierarchies in an effort to cut costs. General managers and top executives may be more affected by these cost-cutting strategies than in the past, thus moderating employment growth.

Although this is a large occupation and many openings will appear each year as executives transfer to other positions, start their own businesses, or retire, competition for top managerial jobs will be keen. Many executives who leave their jobs transfer to other executive or managerial positions, limiting openings for new entrants, and large numbers of layoffs resulting from downsizing and restructuring will lead to an ample supply of competent managers. Moreover, the aging of the workforce will result in more senior middle managers vying for a limited number of top executive positions.

Projected employment growth of general managers and top executives varies widely among industries. For example, employment growth is expected to be faster than average in all services industries combined, but slower than average in all finance, insurance, and real estate industries combined. Employment of general managers and top executives is projected to decline in manufacturing industries overall.

Managers whose accomplishments reflect strong leadership qualities and the ability to improve the efficiency or competitive position of their organizations will have the best opportunities in all industries. In an increasingly global economy, certain types of experience, such as international economics, marketing, or information systems, or knowledge of several disciplines will also be advantageous.

III. Financial Managers

Like other managerial occupations, the number of applicants for financial management positions is expected to exceed the number of job openings, resulting in competition for jobs. Employment of financial managers is expected to increase about as fast as the average for all occupations through the year 2005. In addition, job openings will arise each year as financial managers transfer to other occupations, start their own businesses, or retire. Similar to other managers, most financial managers who leave their jobs seek other positions in their field; relatively few experienced workers leave the occupation permanently each year.

Although the need for skilled financial management will increase due to the demands of global trade, the proliferation of complex financial instruments, and continually changing federal and state laws and regulations, employment growth among financial managers will be tempered by corporate restructuring and downsizing in many industries. Many firms are reducing their ranks of middle managers in an effort to be more efficient and competitive. Similarly, as the banking industry consolidates and banks merge their operations, some financial management positions may be eliminated. These forces will prevent the need for skilled financial managers from resulting in dramatic employment growth.

Many opportunities will still exist for the most skilled, adaptable, and knowledgeable financial managers. Those who keep abreast of the latest financial instruments and changing regulations, and those familiar with a range of financial services, for example, banking, business credit, credit unions, insurance, real estate, and securities, and with data processing and management information systems, will enjoy the best employment opportunities. Developing expertise in a rapidly growing industry, such as health care, also may prove helpful.

IV. Training, and Labor Relations Specialists and Managers

The number of personnel, training, and labor relations specialists and managers is expected to grow faster than the average for all occupations through the year 2005. As in other occupations, job growth among specialists is projected to outpace job growth among managers. In addition, many job openings will result from the need to replace workers who leave this occupation to transfer to other jobs, retire, or leave for other reasons. However, the job market is likely to remain competitive in view of the abundant supply of qualified college graduates and experienced workers.

Most new jobs for personnel, training, and labor relations specialists and managers will be in the private sector as employers will be increasingly concerned about productivity and quality of work, and will devote greater resources to job-specific training programs in response to the growing complexity of many jobs, the aging of the workforce, and technological advances that can leave employees with obsolete skills. In addition, legislation and court rulings setting standards in occupational safety and health, equal employment opportunity, wages, and health, pension, family leave, and other benefits will increase demand for experts in these areas. The increasing cost of litigation related to labor–management disputes may spur demand for labor relations workers to help resolve these disputes out of court. Increasing demand for international human resources managers and human resources information systems specialists may spur additional job growth. On the other hand, widespread use of computerized human resources information systems could make workers more productive, thus limiting job growth.

Employment demand will be particularly strong in management and consulting firms as well as personnel supply firms as businesses increasingly contract out personnel functions or hire personnel specialists on a contractual basis to meet the increasing cost and complexity of training and development programs. Demand should also increase in firms that develop and administer the increasingly complex employee benefits and compensation packages for other organizations.

Demand for personnel, training, and labor relations specialists and managers also is governed by the staffing needs of the firms where they work. A rapidly expanding business is likely to hire additional personnel workers, either as permanent employees or consultants, while a business that has experienced a merger or a reduction in its workforce will require fewer personnel workers. Similar to other workers, employment of personnel, training, and labor relations specialists and managers, particularly in larger firms, may be adversely affected by corporate downsizing and restructuring. On the other hand, as human resource management becomes increasingly important to the success of an organization, some small- and medium-size businesses that do not have a human resources department may employ workers to perform human resources duties on a part-time basis while maintaining other unrelated responsibilities within the company. In any particular firm, the size and the job duties of the human resources staff are determined by a variety of factors, including the firm's organizational philosophy and goals, the labor intensity and skill profile of the industry, the pace of technological change, government regulations, collective bargaining agreements, standards of professional practice, and labor market conditions.

V. Marketing, Advertising, and Public Relations Managers

Employment of marketing, advertising, and public relations managers is expected to increase faster than the average for all occupations through the year 2005. Increasingly intense domestic and global competition in products and services offered to consumers should require greater marketing, promotional, and public relations efforts. Management and public relations firms may experience particularly rapid growth as businesses increasingly hire contractors for these services rather than support additional full-time staff.

In addition to faster than average growth, many job openings will occur each year as a result of managers moving into top management positions, transferring to other jobs, or leaving the labor force. However, many of these highly coveted jobs will be sought by other managers or highly experienced professional and technical personnel, resulting in substantial job competition. College graduates with extensive experience, a high level of creativity, and strong communication skills should have the best job opportunities.

Projected employment growth varies by industry. For example, employment of marketing, advertising, and public relations managers is expected to grow much faster than average in most business services industries, such as computer and data processing, and management and public relations firms, while average growth is projected in manufacturing industries overall.

Appendix II

Communication Studies and Commentaries

P eter Drucker is credited with heeding corporations riding the tremendous wave of change with the following warning: There is a difference between being computer literate and information literate. Taken one step further, there is certainly a difference between being information literate and communication literate, with an increasing number of leading companies espousing the critical importance of the latter competence. A Columbia University study found that 59 percent of CEOs consider frequent communication with employees important to their jobs; 89 percent expect communication to be more important to the CEO's job in the year 2000.

In response to this emerging consensus on the critical power of communication, countless studies have been conducted to investigate what differentiates effective from ineffective practices. We begin this section by previewing two comprehensive studies we feel offer critical lessons to companies that want to create communication strategies that support change through the integration of appropriate media, message, and audience understanding. We then turn to a selection of commentaries by communication, technology, and organizational behavior specialists who echo some of the themes presented throughout this book. The excerpts from books, speeches, and live interviews feature these experts lending their insights into the future communication challenges that lie ahead.

Communication Effectiveness Research

Field Study of Domestic Firms.   Through an in-depth two-year study of ten organizations that lead in communication best practices, Young and Post (1993) delineated eight factors that determine the effectiveness of employee communications during organizational changes. The criteria for successful management of the change initiatives included the degree to which changes were smooth (in the eyes of management), the amount of staff turnover, and the general tone or morale of the managerial and nonmanagerial staff (as reflected in employee surveys). Furthermore, in each of the ten organizations, managers were able to identify quantifiable business measures (sales, profitability, revenue per employee, or other financial measure) used to track organizational performance.

The companies in this study represented a variety of industries and organizational settings, thus increasing the likelihood that the results could be generalized to any number of organizations seeking to enhance the effectiveness of their communication practices. The eight communication-effectiveness factors outlined in the study were as follows:

1. *The chief executive as communications champion.*   The researchers found that if the CEO was not *philosophically* and *behaviorally* committed to leading communication effectiveness, the achievement of corporate goals was affected. Thus, as champions CEOs must firmly believe that communication is a "need to have," not simply a "nice to have." Furthermore, CEOs must be skilled and visible communications role models. Interestingly, even in those cases where the leader was not considered a polished media personality, concerted efforts on the part of the chief executive officer to model these behaviors had a powerful impact as well.

2. *The match between words and actions.*   Plain and simple, talk is cheap and actions speak louder than words. The researchers found that the critical link here was between the messages communicated by the CEO and the resultant managerial actions. Participants in the study reported that it was not unusual for managers to send implicit messages through their behavior that seemingly contradicted the official message that was conveyed in the formal communication from the top. Clearly, official messages can be rendered completely ineffective if managerial actions do not support and complement them.

3. *Commitment to two-way communication.*   Through numerous total-quality and employee involvement programs, dialogue has become an important communication issue. Nevertheless, the study found that actual commitment to this ideology varied greatly throughout organizations. Those that were committed did so enthusiastically and saw great returns on their investment in this effort. Those that were less committed admitted to needing improvement in the area; one company reported on the adverse effect of "not listening enough" to employees during a recent restructuring.

4. *Emphasis on face-to-face communication.* An effective, ongoing practice, the study found, is using face-to-face communication for sensitive issues and especially during times of uncertainty and change. Used in conjunction with other media, this "high-touch" approach made a significant difference in one firm. Through feedback from employees, management learned that the face-to-face encounters had made a critical difference in how it managed a major acquisition.

5. *Shared responsibility for employee communications.* The study found effective organizations underscoring the imperative that every manager is a communications manager. Employees who were polled regarding their preferred venue for receiving critical news responded that hearing it from their manager was most important.

6. *The bad news/good news ratio.* An informal content analysis suggested that this ratio varies widely, with no particular ratio as more effective than another. What did come through was that the free flow of information, including bad news, provides important strategic advantages. One organization that pushed responsibility for reporting problems down to employees positioned the communication of bad news as culturally valued and institutionally important. Moreover, the researchers found that when bad news was reported candidly, an environment was created in which good news was taken as more credible.

7. *Knowing customers, clients, and audiences.* The researchers found that Tom Peters' concept of "keeping close to the customer" was a clear trend in a large number of the companies studied, seen as an insistence that employee communications staff monitor their customers and audiences and understand organizational issues, job demands, and other communications efforts that affect the customer on the receiving end of the message. In the best companies, communications programs serve the audience's needs and, as a result, improve the organization's capacity for dealing with change.

8. *The employee communication strategy.* Among leading companies, employee communications is viewed as a critical management process, beyond the output of communication products, and thus an integral part of effective business strategy. The researchers defined this focus on process as new and delineated the following five consensus ideas from the sample of leading companies: (1) Communicate not only what is happening, but why and how it is happening. (2) Timeliness is vital. (3) Communicate continuously. (4) Link the "big picture" with the "little picture." (5) Don't dictate the way people should feel about the news.

Two surprises that came out of the research was that neither the *size of the employee communications budget* nor the *reporting relationship* emerged as a major influence on the effectiveness of employee communications. While each factor could certainly improve or constrain the rollout of a communication strategy, they do not determine the ability of staff to serve its audiences. It is this *culture for communication* that ultimately differentiates the effective from ineffective practices.

Survey Study of Domestic and International Firms.   In a survey of 110 U.S. and 20 European businesses, The Conference Board (1995) explored the pivotal role that communication campaigns play in supporting and dri- ving change. The prevalence of internal communication efforts related to fourteen change initiatives was investigated (see Figure A2.1).

Seventy percent of the respondents reported that their companies have mounted communication campaigns in at least five of the fourteen change initiatives delineated, and at least one third had addressed each of the fourteen different areas to underscore their capability to deal with change. The priority messages being delivered in those campaigns focused on four parameters:

- Shifts in financial performance
- Corporate strategy
- Vision, and mission, leadership
- Focus on customers

Resulting "increased understanding" was found to be the primary criteria of effectiveness that companies used as benchmarks to weigh the quality of their campaigns. What was more ambitious was the reporting that a majority of communication executives are driving for attitudinal and behavioral changes to occur as a result of the campaigns as well. The communication success factors delineated from this study mirror some of those found by Young and Post (1995), although The Conference Board study examined not only global success factors, but also which factors played the most important role in which types of campaigns (see Figures A2.2 and A2.3).

The five major types of campaigns were characterized as focusing on strategy/vision/mission, new compensation benefits packages, customer focus, CEO/leadership team, and process redesign. The top five factors across all types of internal campaigns, in order of perceived importance, were:

1. Message content
2. Involvement of senior management
3. Strength/cohesion of total campaign strategy
4. Involvement of line management
5. Ease of access to audience

These were followed by opportunity for two-way communication, choice of delivery mechanisms, timing of campaign, research/experience with target audience, duration of effort, adequate campaign budget, and use of outside expertise.

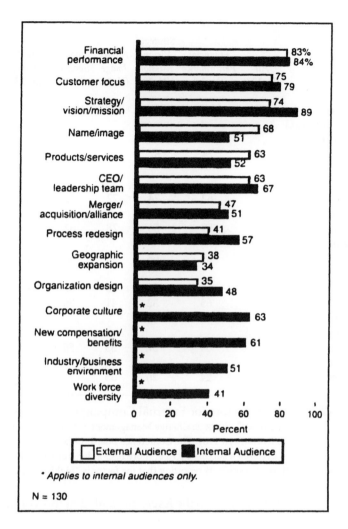

Figure A2.1 Prevalence of communication Efforts To Support Change Initiatives Source: Change Management: Communication's Pivotal Role by Kathryn Troy. The Conference Board, 1995

Commentaries

The New Landscape. At the 1995 annual meeting of the Electronic Messaging Association, Jim Manzi, then CEO of Lotus Development Corporation, made a keynote presentation (May 8, 1995) in which he described the changing role of information systems in today's business organization.

	All (N=127)	Financial Performance (N=29)	Strategy/ Vision/ Mission (N=19)	Name/ Image (N=17)	Products Services (N=16)	M&A/ Alliances (N=13)	CEO/ Leadership Team (N=10)
Message content ...	97%	100%	95%	88%	100%	100%	100%
Strength/cohesion of total campaign strategy	81	74	87	88	80	92	60
Research/ experience with target audience	66	62	74	72	81	46	70
Choice of delivery mechanisms	62	59	56	78	62	77	50
Timing of campaign	58	69	68	33	56	77	60
Ease of access to audience	56	55	58	50	62	61	60
Duration of effort ...	52	65	32	41	56	50	40
Adequate campaign budget	38	34	37	53	50	25	20
Use of outside expertise	24	24	26	35	12	38	—

Figure A2.2 Success Factors for External Compaigns (by Type of Initiative)* SOURCE: Change Management: Communication's Pivotal Role by Kathryn Troy. The Conference Board, 1995

*Only those intitiatives declared a success by 10 or more respondents are included. Percentages indicate those respondents reporting that the factor is "highly" important.

Portions of the speech relevant to the issues presented in this volume are presented below:

> There has been a wealth of commentary and insight on how the structure of the business organization is changing—from hierarchical, command and control models, to structures that are flatter, leaner, faster, and decentralized. And it's generally acknowledged that technology—specifically information technology—is driving this change.
>
> But even though the change is being driven by information technology, far less attention has been paid to the changing role of what used to be called MIS in the new organizational structure. I believe that in the new networked organization the essential task is no longer one of information management, but one of communications management.
>
> And I think it's becoming clear that communications management can no longer be considered a support function, but has emerged front and center as

	All (N=127)	Strategy/ Vision/ Mission (N=27)	New Compensation Benefits Package (N=16)	Customer Focus (N=14)	Leadership Team (N=10)	CEO/ Process Redesign (N=10)
Message content ...	95%	96%	100%	93%	90%	90%
Involvement of senior management	88	100	56	93	100	100
Strength/cohesion of total campaign strategy	82	92	80	85	75	90
Involvement of line management ...	73	74	69	93	50	90
Ease of access to audience	70	70	62	54	70	80
Opportunity for two-way communication	69	73	81	73	60	60
Choice of delivery mechanisms	60	58	56	64	50	70
Timing of campaign .	60	67	62	29	80	70
Research/experience with target audience	59	56	69	71	40	50
Duration of effort ...	52	50	50	60	40	60
Adequate campaign budget	30	35	44	43	20	10
Use of outside expertise	17	15	31	14	10	20

Figure A2.3 Success Factors for Internal Compaigns (by Type of Initiative)* SOURCE: Change Management: Communication's Pivotal Role by Kathryn Troy. The Conference Board, 1995

*Only those intitiatives declared a success by 10 or more respondents are included. Percentages indicate those respondents reporting that the factor is "highly" important.

the key priority of top management—not MIS, but management period, as in CEOs and senior management. It's their job to provide the infrastructure and help manage complexity in a decentralized organization.

Let me begin with my more controversial first point on how messaging is changing, and evolving into groupware. I mentioned how messaging has evolved through four distinct stages—from simple text to complex objects with links.

I think you can view this evolution in terms of two fundamental, and quite different, approaches to how all of us get our information.

The first is the push model. It includes traditional, physical mail delivery, as in Benjamin Franklin, the U.S. Postal Service, and the Pony Express. E-mail is a newer, more technologically advanced push model. It is superior because it overcomes barriers not just of space, but also time. And there can be no question about its success. Many businesses will tell you that they do not know how they were able to get along in the world before e-mail. We tend to forget how recent it is. There are people today whose business cards include their e-mail address, but not their phone number.

But despite its great success and recent origin, e-mail nonetheless conforms to the classical push model: I decide that you need to see something, or you have asked me for something and I push it into your space. But one of the problems, of course, is there is more and more mail, and the envelopes are getting bigger and bigger. I'm sure that most of you are no different than I am, and I now get about 200 e-mails a day.

I can filter out some, but you don't want to be too restrictive and cut yourself off from people who may be pushing something important at you. There is also a kind of social contract involved with e-mail. When someone has sent something to you, there is an implicit obligation to respond—even more so than with letters. A week ago I received an interesting resume via e-mail and when I hadn't replied within 4 days, I then got a flame-o-gram, which tended to undercut the resume. The social contract can quite clearly run into problems of scale.

The overload applies not just to users, but to the network as well, with mail now taking up a greater and greater proportion of network capacity. Ten years ago the relevant measurement for the size of a messaging system was the number of users. Five years ago you kept track by the number of messages per week. Today the size of messaging systems is measured in the number of gigabytes per day.

I talked recently to one customer that accumulates 12 gigabytes a day in mail traffic. That's life today in the network.

Let me offer some personal insight on how quickly it can add up. In the course of a routine business day last month, I was personally responsible for putting 100 megs onto our network within a couple hours. I had prepared a presentation, and since it was for a less sophisticated audience than this one, it also included some visual aids. It was about one meg. I wanted a critique from our people before giving it, so I sent it out to 10 people.

At Lotus, and probably at most companies, there are two things that always happen when you do this. First, there is a compulsion to find something that must be changed—even if it's a typo on page 13. And second, social protocol demands that you not only inform me, but also everyone else about the typo on page 13. So you hit the reply all key, and after everyone else has done the same thing, my modest one meg work-in-progress has become 100 megs on the network.

Consider the same multiplier when it is a new marketing campaign that's being sent out for comment or when my text and slide attachment becomes a video. As more people collect more things in bigger and bigger envelopes, and push them out on the wire, it simply doesn't scale.

The other approach to getting information is the pull model. Everything is out there in databases, and all you must do is go out and get it—pull it in. A library is the classic pull model. Over the past 10 to 15 years, the most dramatic electronic version of the pull model has been the remarkable growth of the World Wide Web. The Web was thriving long before the Internet made the cover of *Newsweek*.

The pull model is essentially a database model. The classic pull model has its own obvious limitations. From the users' standpoint, it is the old problem of information overload. In a vast sea of information, how do I get the information I really need? It's entirely possible to starve to death in the great cornucopia of the Web.

The pull model has its own set of social obligations, or rules of engagement. Since all this information is now out there, and accessible at 14.4 baud or higher—virtually at my finger tips—there is an obligation to log on and go traipsing through it. Build it and they will come.

But what if this field of dreams includes, as it does for me, about 500 Notes databases that surely include some information that I can use, and lord knows how many other Web sites where there is at least a high probability of something that is useful? How do I get it? Or, how long will it take me to get to it? Agent technology can help. There are now Web crawlers and spiders that can be programmed to do my bidding.

Not too long ago, anyone who pretended to be a corporate executive would receive something called a decision memo. It would list the pros and cons for a particular action, and there would be three boxes to check—typically something like proceed, kill, or wait. But it's far more useful, if instead of the highly filtered, and probably slanted, listings of the pros and cons, you have instead a pointer that will take you to the previous discussions of the proposed action. You may learn just how the issue originated, and whether the proposed action addresses a real problem or opportunity.

The standard discussions of groupware revolve around the three Cs: communication, collaboration, and coordination. I think it's the third of these—coordination—that is really the key.

Communication is basic, but it's also very broad. When I was here two years ago, I quoted Norbert Weiner saying that communication is the very basis for society—whether it's human society or bees. In the terms of our discussion, communication is simple messaging—moving an object from one person to another. Absolutely fundamental, but obviously not the same thing as groupware, which has not been around nearly as long as human society or bees.

Collaboration is also fundamental to groupware. But when we consider it in terms of today's electronic universe, collaboration means creating space for human interaction—as in a bulletin board or a CompuServe forum. There is something passive about it. No doubt a lot of useful interaction goes on, but the question is: useful to whom, and to what purpose?

I believe that coordination gets us to the heart of groupware because the notion of goals or purpose is implicit. It imposes process on the system, and thereby serves real world business processes—such as developing a product, providing service to a customer, or getting a loan.

This forces a redefinition of what we mean by a transaction. In the database world, transaction has a rather precise and technical definition. It is a set of events that transforms a database from one consistent state to another. It is something that happens in a matter of milliseconds, and it is internal consistency rather than any goal or outcome that really matters. What are our current prices? How many seats on today's flights are now available?

But if you were to say to your average business person—not a database administrator—that a transaction is "a set of events that transforms a database from one consistent state to another," you would very likely get a quizzical, blank stare.

In business, a transaction is doing a deal. It happens over time, and may involve such things as market research, targeting customers, discussions with customers, and negotiating a price. It is a series of events that may include many different people, different parts of the organization—often different organizations—and it is directed towards a goal.

If we take the business definition of a transaction, then groupware must include a heavy component of workflow. You can start with simple workflow—something as mundane as ordering pencils, which is a real world business process that involves more than issuing a purchase order. It begins with someone who wants the pencils, and it ends when he gets the pencils— and the steps in between should be as automatic and painless as possible.

But it also includes more serious tasks, such as hiring a new employee. Ideally, the information flow should be structured to reflect company policies, legal obligations, and past experience. Workflow also applies to other serious issues like product development, where current intelligence becomes part of a structural flow of information that leads to a better outcome—namely, better products.

The biggest danger of workflow has always been potential rigidity. It has been pointed out that even though Mussolini made the trains run on time, there are other considerations. Obviously, markets change, goals change, and processes themselves must be subject to change. That's why rapid application development is key to workflow, and absolutely crucial if groupware is to achieve its full impact in an organization. What's required is a continuum of development tools, and a rich development environment for a broad range of users.

What does this mean for central IS? What is its role, if suddenly we have all these PC users out there on the network who are writing their own applications? Is this really what we mean by integrated messaging? It would appear to be disintegration, and would appear to diminish the importance of IS.

But it is actually just the opposite. As I mentioned at the outset, the changing structure of business organizations—away from the hierarchical pyramid and towards decentralization—brings IS front and center, with new and much broader responsibilities. It has to do with increased complexity.

There is no denying the roles of telecommunications and the microprocessor in bringing about what I call the deconstruction of the American corporation.

The reason is the primacy of speed. A number of years ago Daniel Bell published some research on the impact of technology on cycle time (the conception to delivery of a product or service). In the early part of this century, it took 30 years to get a product to market, but it had fallen to less than a third of that by 1967. Since then, the impact of technology and speed has become even more dramatic. Cycle time is now three years in some industries, 18 months in others, and 9 months in parts of the PC industry.

The primacy of speed places new demands on corporate organizations to gather market and competitive information like never before. There is a need for information from the periphery, or far reaches of the organization, if you will—for which computer networks are ideally suited.

So naturally—even if naturally in this case means dramatically—a new networked organization is replacing the older forms—driven by technology. It has the advantages of flexibility, closeness to markets, and speed of response, but it is also more complex—some would say chaotic. The challenge is to achieve a coordinated enterprise that operates according to network rules we establish.

I have come to view this as the ability to decentralize risk and risk-taking within our enterprises—to move it away from the center and out toward the market, toward the customer.

How to distribute risk to the periphery while managing and reducing complexity from the center has become the key global–local issue for today's corporation. The guiding principle, as Einstein says, is simple as possible, but not too simple.

The new networked organization is based on the distribution of knowledge, intelligence, thinking, and risk taking. In fact, it is a redistribution of these same powers that was extracted towards the center in the hierarchical organization.

The task of management in the networked organization becomes one of coordination, clarification, setting some rules, and a strategic agenda. It becomes part of the job of management to see that risk is distributed, but according to rules and within a new network infrastructure.

The most successful companies already know this. The reigning philosophy at 3M, which has achieved legendary status for its innovation and product development, is that mistakes made by people close to the market will never be as serious as those made by central management. In a sense, the risks are more bite sized.

Earlier this year, I visited with a top executive of ABB, which is a $30 billion global engineering company with something like 1,200 business units. They manage operations in 30 countries around the world with a central management consisting of just 150 people in Zurich. The job of central management comes down to three things: strategic direction, technology infrastructure, and training.

Infrastructure is key to managing complexity. The role of central management is to capitalize on the benefits of technology and counter the iatrogenic effects—the tendency for the cure to be worse than the disease.

The role of the center in a networked organization becomes communications management—not information management. Information management alone has become the corporate equivalent of undertaking. Information by itself is inert, impersonal, Cartesian, and nonpurposive. It has less value to the organization. It is based mostly on what's already occurred. Communications, on the other hand, is dynamic, vibrant and future oriented. It is the process by which intelligence and know-how are mobilized in a networked organization. It is about what the organization wants to do or is trying to be.

The corporate republic (a word I chose carefully because it invokes notions of citizenship and responsibility) based on the networked organization is still a work in progress. Many issues remain.

One is how to scale human relations in a decentralized, networked organization. As Michael Schrage has pointed out, when the central task is no longer information management, it becomes communications management, which is the equivalent of relationship management. This leads to larger questions, such as, how do you deal with human sentiment in a digital age? (or, can a newsgroup on the Internet replace the local Elks Club?). Or how do you deal with those social obligations or rules of engagement I mentioned earlier, which quickly run into problems of scale?

The breakdown of old structures and the emergence of new ones inevitably involves the search for metaphors. And in the new networked organization there is no getting away from the concept of teams—even though it suffers from rhetorical excess.

Even so, as corporations deconstruct, what they are deconstructing into is teams. Innovation demands it because the team is the optimal unit of the techno-commercial imagination. Quality control demands it because the team is the largest practical unit of collective responsibility. And human nature takes to teams because we are gregarious by nature. And it is this reliance on teams that is helping drive the convergence of messaging and groupware.

The ultimate challenge of the networked organization is to forge the ties among teams and to the larger organization—a kind of dual citizenship—that is the only sure basis for any successful organization. These larger ties cannot be simply economic, but must be ties of sentiment and value. In a digital age and in an age where old structures are breaking down, shared values have become more important than ever. This, too, has become part of the challenge for IS—not just how people relate to technology, but how people relate to people using technology.

Leadership in the New Landscape. The following excerpt is from Dr. Teery Bacon's *Leading the Virtual Corporation* (Copyright, All Rights Reserved October 1995), in which Dr. Bacon outlines some of the hard realities, the challenges and opportunities inherent in the emerging virtual structure. He also discusses the competencies and perspectives required for effectively leading and managing such an environment.

Traditional corporate structure is changing. Companies large and small are utilizing more independent contractors, and permanent part time employees. Outsourcing is no longer a trend, but a corporate religion practiced even in situations where it may not make complete sense.

Underlying these and other externally visible trends is an underlying movement by firms towards increasing reliance on "self managers," skilled employees and contractors who accomplish their tasks with far less guidance and supervision than previously thought possible. The shift towards a "virtual" corporation is real and far reaching, and should have forward-looking managers asking: "How would one lead a virtual corporation?"

Today, most "self managers" are the "knowledge professionals" defined in Peter Drucker's 1972 book *Management*. Tomorrow self-management practices are likely to encompass workers at all levels of firms. When you combine enabling communication technologies like e-mail with a trend toward a self-managing workforce you experience increasing corporate "Virtualization," the changing of a corporation's identity from that of a physical building or manufacturing facility to a interconnected network of individuals and subcontractors who all work for "themselves." A truly "virtual" corporation of any size, lacking even a corporate headquarters building, will probably never exist any more than the "paperless" office does. A "virtual" corporation might develop within the same four walls a traditional corporation occupies. But this evolution, this "virtualization" will greatly affect what goes on within those walls.

The impetus for the virtual corporation is a change in mindset of the American worker. Employees today are demanding greater autonomy. Relaxed dress codes, flex-hours, and family leave are external manifestations of this change. It's not merely a Generation X phenomenon, but a desire by greater numbers of workers at all levels to be self governing and have more input into how they do their jobs. After all, who knows how to do the job better than the person actually doing it? Managers had better get used to that idea even if their corporations refuse to formally acknowledge it. Properly managed this emerging desire for self-management can lead to tremendous gains in efficiency. Both employee and customer satisfaction can improve. Unmanaged, or resisted, it can lead to increased employee turnover, and employees intentionally sabotaging corporate efforts/goals?: "If I can't do it my way I'll make sure yours doesn't work!"

Fueling the change in corporate structure is the fact that fewer firms today are able to offer lifetime employment. Many individuals can become more secure by specializing, and selling their skills from home than by working for big corporations. Even the future of mega-corporations like IBM or GM have become increasingly uncertain. The virtual annihilation of the Defense industry left tens of thousands of workers hanging, workers whose years of loyalty to firms like LTV and what is now Lockheed Martin came to be worth almost nothing. Becoming self employed, and ever after "true (only) to yourself" became an exceedingly attractive option for many of these laid off workers. Instead of lifetime employment, or even the more statistically truthful changing of jobs every 2.3 years independent contractors simply "suit up" and go out and find new sources of work when one source dries up. Loyalty has little or nothing to do with it. It's an economic relationship, conducted at arms length, between independent contractors and the firms that hire them. Pure and simple. So many units of output for so many dollars.

The widespread adoption of new technologies like e-mail, fax, and overnight package delivery service enabled the homeward movement of many knowledge professionals. Technology is helping to catalyze corporate "virtualization." Groupware applications like Lotus Notes, for instance, will allow entire groups of individuals to collaborate on the same document simultaneously, even from homes and offices scattered around the globe. Leading a virtual corporation will require mastering these new communication paths, as well as helping to further develop the new infrastructure. We may see the heads of MIS departments moving into line for CEO positions in the future. The widespread adoption of e-mail as an inter- and intra-company messaging system has radically altered corporate communication paths. E-mail has had the effect of flattening the corporate hierarchy. Employees not comfortable walking into the President's office may feel completely comfortable zipping off a brief e-mail about something troubling them, or submitting a suggestion about a better way to do their job. A lot of meetings have been eliminated by the appropriate use of e-mail's "carbon copy" feature. Agreement and consensus can now be sought with everyone remaining in their respective offices. E-mail has truly revolutionized how corporate individuals communicate; the term corporate requiring strenuous re-definition as "Individuals united into one body or collective or collaborating on a task or goal."

The corporate structure likely to result from virtualization will be a hybrid; employing both telecommuting independent contractors and those employees who prefer the traditional office and the synergy working in direct contact with others offers. Faster processors, multi-media kits, and new conferencing standards will soon allow individuals to use their PC's as video telephones, allowing on-line face to face contact. The Internet, and these new communications technologies will serve as powerful catalysts to significant changes in corporate communication channels.

How do you manage individuals in the new structure? The truth is that traditional carrot and stick principles of blue collar management won't work any better for today's telecommuting contractors and "self managers" than they did for the predominantly white collar work force that emerged in 1972. Having the people skills to motivate and financial authority to reward self-managers will be critical to the virtual leader. Independent contractors often work for several "bosses" at the same time.

Changing employers can be done quickly and easily, without considerations like relocation. The implication for the manager is that he'd better continually make sure his contractors feel appreciated and rewarded for their efforts. On the flip side, it's much easier to hire and fire in the virtual corporation. A manager will no longer live in fear of government rules and lawsuits that kept them from letting an individual go after reviewing their actual performance. You fire an independent contractor by simply not giving them any more work. In the hands of a good manager this can quickly lead to a higher quality organization. Does this mean that contractors should be given no room for failure, no margin of error? No.

Self-managing contractors can quickly sense which managers care about them and their needs. They will all want to work for "Joe," who asks about their kids and tries to ensure they are supplied enough work to make their tuition payments, and will subconsciously steer themselves away from "Bob" whose only concern is "Bob's project" and "Bob's schedule."

Individuals who have succeeded in positions requiring self management skills, whether as independent contractors working at home or in an office lacking middle management don't require supervision per se.

What they really need is leadership. The only "manager" most such individuals will consent to work for is a cheerleader, a mentor, a resource gatherer or someone with some combination of these qualities. This manager must also be a friend, someone who can empathize and understand their lifestyle, rather than someone who resents it or is jealous of the telecommuting contractor. The virtual leader must be out gathering resources needed by individuals already working for the virtual corporation as well as gathering up the individuals themselves; identifying and recruiting the self-employed contractors, the support staff, and the outsourced service firms that together effect the virtual corporation.

Industry will look for the leaders who can attract the most talent that least likes (and sometimes least fits into) the traditional corporate structure, but thrives in a "virtual" corporation. Gathering these "human resources," and animating them with the vision of a viable, mutually beneficial future resulting from cooperating on a shared "corporate" goal is the virtual leader's job. The virtual corporation will be a combination of hardware, software, and humanware.

Comparing the "virtual" economy to an agrarian economy, the tele-commuting independent contractor has been compared to the family farmer of old. The farmer is the ultimate example of a self-manager. He/she decides which fields offer the most fertile plowing, and what to plant. In the virtual corporation, the leader's job becomes convincing self-managing sharecroppers to work his corporate fields for their mutual benefit.

In the agricultural analogy, the virtual "leader" might also be compared to a county agricultural agent—a mentor of sorts. The farmer knows his fields, his crops; he or she usually knows their animals personally. The agent knows his chemistry, animal husbandry, and has specialized training that can help the farmer get even more corn out of an acre of land. He also benefits from knowing what everyone else is doing. He may be able to offer the "big picture" to someone intently focused on the "back forty."

The best managers in the virtual corporation will be those able to help these self-managing individuals achieve more than they believed they themselves were capable of. The leader of the "virtual corporation," like a preacher or visionary, is tasked with creating belief: Employees' belief in themselves and their talents, belief in a prosperous vision of the future. The power of encouragement by a leader was never better illustrated than when Napoleon said, "With a chest of medals, I can win a war." In the virtual corporation it may be an e-mail of congratulations.

The virtual manager must be capable of motivating the no-collar worker to seek rewards beyond the tremendous freedom of working for one's self, and instill in them the quest of achieving larger goals that can only be reached through incorporation with other individuals. This will require investing significant effort to understand each self managing employee's personal aspirations. And recognizing self-managers efforts publicly may be somewhat more challenging since there is no Monday meeting or water cooler around which to casually mention John or Mary's recent achievement, although a Monday morning on-line chat may suffice.

What are the challenges facing the leaders of the virtual or "no-collar" corporation? There will be a tremendous sense of loss of control for those who cannot "Hang on loosely." They will be forced to adopt, and even create new ways of monitoring progress. "Walk-around" management will need to transition to something new, perhaps "Surf around—via Internet." Or even making house calls on home workers. The no-collar manager may often wonder who is working for who as they keep their self-managing workers supplied with the resources and encouragement needed to keep them motivated. Good managers of old may very well become discouraged seeing other individuals better suited to the new corporate culture. Recognizing one's talents and limitations will definitely be required of the no-collar manager to avoid discouragement

The "virtual" manager will need to be able to write clearly, so that e-mails, which will substitute for a large number of previously voice conversations, are clear, and can't be misconstrued. The virtual manager will have to be a master of building relationships. The virtual corporation is dependent on relationships. Independent contracting smears the artificial division between personal and business relationships. The virtual corporation cannot thrive without leaders who can form and nurture relationships, creating "friends" of the business whose own networks can bring good to the "corporation."

A major role for the leader of the virtual corporation will be that of creating community; bringing his or her people together both in cyberspace and in person. The leader must make all of the players feel like part of a team, creating the sense of belonging that these new communication paths tend to destroy. Working at home, on any extended assignment away from the home office, can sometimes make one feel as if one has been left abandoned on a deserted island, void of human contact outside of pure business communications—brief, to the point e-mails. The leader must occasionally gather the flock together, emotionally, if not physically, through award ceremonies, sales meetings, product launches, and other corporate "rituals" which strengthen the "working together" mentality so vital for success. He or she must create an "artificial" water cooler to allow the personal connections and relationship building to take place, whether this is through mandatory picnics, "training" sessions, or whatever. It can't be "all business" all the time or self-managers will "burn out" of working for a particular corporation and go in search of a "friendlier" one.

Some of the most effective corporate structures have traditionally been informal networks. This isn't going to change in the virtual corporation. From these informal networks new "virtual managers" may arise.

The leaders of today's corporations need to observe the traffic on the network, so to speak, and see which managers can "surf," riding the technological and cultural changes virtualization brings. The leader must become more of a conveyer of information than a controller if he or she is to succeed, since virtualization causes the destruction of some forms of communication—like the water cooler and hallway conversations.

"Consensus" managers may have a tough time in the virtual corporation since there won't be as many meetings in which you can sense which way the wind is blowing. They will be required to make more decisions on their own or based only on e-mailed advice from a select few. A leader will also be someone who embraces the new technology, and information, and supplies their protégé's with plentiful access to it. Many draftsmen retired when CAD tools started replacing drafting boards. The same thing will happen with the new tools and communication paths, but for a whole class of information managers and employees, not just a select group of design specialists.

Within both the old, and the virtual corporation, the leader must be willing to take calculated risks and step off the beaten path. The leader must be able to gather a critical mass of support for a new project from people one step lower in the (formal) hierarchy, who themselves are able to bring people aboard from below that. These "recruitees" can come either from within the corporation, or from self-manager's personal networks. Convincing intelligent, independent, self-managers to "get on board" will be twice as difficult "Leave your fields, your farm, and your family business behind," he orates; "And come sharecrop for me." Only a firm belief in the no-collar leader will suffice, for independent contractors are usually equally happy following their own visions, satisfying their own needs.

The only firms that are going to survive a transition to a "virtual" corporate structure are those who identify, and support those managers capable of recruiting, leading, and encouraging self-managing individuals. A business "unit" made up largely of self-managing telecommuters, independent contractors, and a leader emotionally capable of the "hang on loosely" tasks of directing, supporting, and encouraging all of them will perhaps together form the most efficient corporate structure ever devised, but only for those leaders who are willing to cross the clearing of uncertainty that moving into the future requires. And who knows? Maybe someday there actually will be a "virtual" corporation with no building, and no salaried or hourly employees. It will exist purely on paper, on Internet, and in the minds of the individuals who form the corporation.

Followership in the New Landscape.   The following excerpt is from Chris Houston and Morrey Ewing's book, *Leadership in the Virtual Corporation*, in which the authors discuss place, role, and identity issues employees must manage while working within a virtual environment.

The virtual world, as many experience it, is a world without traditional borders. Information flows instantaneously. Incentive systems unceasingly signal what our behavior just was and what it should be next. Every customer need must be identified, leapt upon, serviced and responded to without delay. Roles, responsibilities, skills, and alliances shift continuously—becoming what they must become today to get the job done yesterday! We are faced with the most demanding and fastest moving customers ever known, and we believe that the virtual enterprise is best suited to offer these customers products uniquely tailored to their needs. Products designed, delivered, and supported when, where, and how the customer wants it. The virtual enterprise may seem to offer an alluring world, but how many of us are genuinely keen to be part of it? What is there in it to sustain the human spirit? What could there be? In a nutshell, the only thing that will redeem, or convict, the organization of the future in the eyes of its employees will be the presence or absence of strong, personal, trusting relationships. The virtual world demands trust between partners, among team members and within alliances. It promotes and relies on trust between suppliers and customers. Such trust is a powerful force for change, bridging competitive barriers and exploding generations of isolationist thinking. Remarkably, this trust springs, not from a contract, but from persons who give it away, freely. In the old days, bureaucracies offered comforting roles, rules, and operating procedures to shelter employees from the rigors of unfriendly employers or uncertain markets. In the new, virtual organization, the needs of both the organization and its people can be met only when leaders focus on building trusting relationships. Let's look at today's virtual enterprise and examine its impact on some of the people in it.

The first person we see is standing alone asking: "Where do I belong?" Call him Peter. His is the dilemma of place. He's been an employee of a financial services company that has told him that he is now "an independent business." If he'd wanted to be independent he wouldn't have chosen to be an employee, waiting for instructions from his manager. Peter doesn't want to be a franchise. For Peter, the company has lost its way and so has he.

The second person we see stands guard over an endless assortment of spare parts—cogs, wheels, and rollers—each with a function, yet each disconnected from the others. "What is my job?" he asks himself. His is the dilemma of role. Let's call him Ron. He leads the key product businesses in a large multinational. He's built a flourishing business. Now he needs alliances internally and externally. His skills at control and enforcement seem useless in building teams. The new enterprise, consisting of a closely coupled supplier network, simply cannot continue to function with Ron insisting on making all decisions himself. Ron wants his sandbox. He badly needs to reach out to the research community and the sales force and draw them into the planning and innovation process. But that is not who he is. Ron's traditional role has been to control functions. Why is role so important? Surely our role is just a performance? But many of us become fiercely possessive of our role, for it assures us of who we are. The virtual world demands that we adapt our roles. It challenges, fundamentally, who we are.

Third, we see a group of faceless statues. Whether they are together or not, we cannot tell. Unable to recognize or be recognized, each bears a sign that reads "Who am I?" Theirs is the dilemma of identity. Are they a group or are they individuals? They are both, and that is the crux of this dilemma. Are we individuals or are we community? The virtual world gives us two equally strong and yet powerfully conflicting signals. Ron is an individualist, a proud one and successful in the past, but now he needs to submit his individualism to the team, to a community of suppliers and trade customers. The virtual world is driven inexorably to satisfy the unique needs of each customer. Why build an alliance for a competence you don't have? To take advantage of a market opportunity. Why integrate as a supplier with your customer? To more effectively satisfy their unique needs. The virtual organization is a response to the demands of individuals. Modern commerce began with mass markets and gradually focused on market segments, but in the virtual world it ends up with a batch size of one. The virtual organization has developed to serve customers one at a time. But it depends upon a community in which individuals no longer define themselves as "I" but rather as "we." When we consume, we are celebrated as "individual" but when we produce, we must become "we." The forces of individualism can only be served by the cohesion of community and the solitudes that result from this contradiction can only create more tensions for those who live in the virtual organization.

Down the hall from Ron is Jennifer, a relationship manager. She scours the company in search of the rare talent she needs to build a team to create a brand new business within a business. Jennifer doesn't choose people on the basis of the roles they have played. She doesn't want employees' numbers, she wants them. Jennifer is succeeding because she's building relationships one person at a time. The key is trust, and if we are to build trusting relationships in the virtual organization, as persons we must begin with authenticity.

We have to explode the myth that we can separate our business lives from our personal lives. In the virtual organization, with its dependence on relationships, business has become personal. Trust requires it and the virtual organization will not thrive without it. We live in a world so competitive that to be authentic is to risk uncomfortable disclosure. It's like relationship "chicken"—who will give trust first? Not who will get it, but who will give it? Partners and functions need to disclose information they have kept secret. If customers and suppliers are to fully collaborate, someone will have to share "secret" information first. Even cost data will end up on the table, or the value chain cannot be optimized along its entire length. It is one thing to disclose cost information and product concepts, it is a far greater challenge to disclose oneself to another so that trust can build. This leads not only to trust in partners, but to friendship itself. And it is friendship which transcends commerce and gives meaning to work.

Effective leaders in the virtual organization must be able to draw on personal experience. Those who have not learned from major personal change cannot help others to find their own solutions. What boundaries do you have to cross before you ask others to follow? In what state are your relationships with your own people or among your suppliers or customers? Do you have bridges to cross or wounds to heal before you can display the kind of behavior you are asking for from others? As the leaders grow, so grows the organization.

Mercifully we do not need to resolve the dilemmas alone. The virtual world, with its intricate network of trust relationships, offers the support of community. Community depends on a mutuality of accountability and nobody wants to be shackled by another. The irony is that the market will give us little choice. To deliver excellent, customized service demands such a high level of integration, collaboration, inter-dependence, and mutuality of objectives from such a diverse and varied source of skills and assets that we must live in community. How we deal with the dilemma of identity will largely determine whether we are significant contributors in the virtual world.

Will we succumb to the "I" of North American individualism or submerge ourselves in the "we" of networked communities? Some will not make the trip from individualist to person.

So how are leaders to move their organizations forward? They can learn to watch and listen to how their people experience the virtual world. To what extent has place, role, or even identity been shaken by the changes they are living through? In listening, leaders can start to build the trust on which the journey forward depends and demonstrate the depth of their concern. Best of all, they need not try to solve it all for everyone. It is enough to work with their people to help them find their own solutions, to help them build trust-filled organizations where such solutions are possible. Only then can we reconcile the needs of the virtual marketplace with our personal needs for a place, a role, and an identity.

The Challenges of the New Landscape.   The following section outlines excerpts from an interview conducted with Elizabeth Allen, the Chief

Executive Officer of International Association of Business Communicators (IABC). The discussion focuses on the emerging corporate communications issues and those with which organizations will need to grapple in the future.

Q: *What are the central issues with respect to electronic media and internal employee communications?*

ALLEN: I think the topic that you've picked for the theme of the book is really a central issue: the flattening of the organization, the breakdown of hierarchy, moving from the traditional organizational chart to the neural or network-like structure, and what that means to internal communications in particular when your employees have the expectations that I think that customers do from an organization in terms of speed, responsiveness, and customized information.

And yet that's not typically the way organizations treat employees. There's essentially, I think, the same power shift going on among employees that there is among customers for an organization, trying to shift from a model of communication that really suited the hierarchical organization to a model that suits the network-like organization. You're really shifting from a one-to-many model to a many-to-many model or receiver-driven model and that can turn an organization on its head if that's not the type of culture that it has had. So there's a strong cultural shift that comes into play and that's a central issue for IABC members who are communicators, who really understand and think through the implications of that and how to manage it.

They have to change their mindsets and perhaps the mindsets of management from controlling information and maybe even gatekeeping information to sharing information and allowing for openness and disclosure, and that's the only way you can really make a network, a neural structure, for an organization work.

Your working in a variety of different teams, you've got to share the information and be more open, and that's often not the mindset of an hierarchical organization.

Q: *Can you cite some examples?*

ALLEN: Certainly. Electronic communication is a tool that most organizations are using these days and the issue is how that tool affects the culture. We interviewed John Perry Barlow (who founded the Electronic Frontier Foundation) for our *Communicator World*. In the article he said e-mail has a way of going through a corporate organization chart like meat tenderizer.

On the one hand, organizations might bring in something like e-mail, and say, "Great, isn't this enhancing our communication," not thinking about the impact on the culture and what it means when lots of folks can communicate with each other independently on their own and access information, and probably ask tougher questions and expect speedy answers.

And I think for the communicator the issue becomes, "How do you facilitate that? You can't necessarily control it. But how do you facilitate it?" I know there's been lots of conversations on some of our online discussion groups that we have of IABC members about setting up an e-mail, what kinds of guidelines you give people for the type of information, and some organizations are saying, "If you've got bad news, you don't deliver it by e-mail, you do it in person." They've had to come up with almost a new etiquette for it.

Information overload. Sifting through, sorting through, and with all the information that's available, what's most important to give people. So decisions about how to organize information for people and distribute it to them.

Also, what do you do if not everybody is able to be online, how do you choose the right media and kind of living life in the parallel zone, offering the same information in many different ways, if you're dealing with a pretty decentralized organization, or an organization that perhaps has a lot of subsidiaries. What do you do when not everyone has the same access?

I think privacy typically comes up. What's going to be the organization's position about the privacy of e-mail, voice-mail? That also comes up.

Q: *What is the impact of e-mail and websites on what has now become traditional electronic media, for example., videotape, videoconferencing?*

ALLEN: I see it as not necessarily taking away from those other areas, but enhancing those other areas. From my perspective our members are just now starting to get into this issue of what medium when and what mix to use. So I don't see that the introduction of some of these other electronic media has yet taken away from the traditional, but it might in the future. Frankly, I think the economy had more to do with taking away a lot of big video departments and a lot of organizations that used to do a lot of television work. But I'm beginning to hear that it's coming back in-house. "It" being even a communication department. The video, I'm hearing, that's not coming back. I am hearing that stripped-down communications departments are starting to build back. I understand that Wells Fargo here in San Francisco has recently done that. They went from 15 down to just a handful and now they're building back up again. They found that they couldn't do what they needed to do as an organization without the communications staff to support it.

Q: *Where do you think it's going?*

ALLEN: I think there's always going to be a place for print. Our members have a visceral attachment to print. They grew up with print. And a lot of managers did. And you have a bit of the conflict potentially between text-trained managers and light-trained employees, for example, trained on computers with not much print. That's another issue to deal with as you get the newer generations of employees coming into an organization, have different expectations as to how they'll receive information.

I think that for another generation or so of management–workforce relationships there's going to have to be a mixture of electronic communication and print communication. The joke I use around here is there are at least three good reasons for retaining print and that's bed, bath, and bus. I find that if I get a long e-mail message, I'll print it out and read it when it gets over some magic number of words or paragraphs, I don't know what it is, but if you find too much, don't have the time, print it out and read it later.

It's the communicator's job to really sort that out, and I think we don't have good answers yet on when to use which medium for what purpose.

The traditional media and electronic media are probably going to be blended at some point into the little box that can do it all—show you the video of the CEO at the annual meeting plus the text, plus give you an e-mail connection to somebody else to answer more questions.

Q: *What about the impact of electronic media on the role of the corporate communicator?*

ALLEN: Huge impact when you think you're operating in, if you believe the Tofflers, a knowledge economy, an information economy. And information becomes the key factor in production. Then the communicator is really trading in the key factor in the economic system. And their role, though, can't be as a gatekeeper of information. The mindset has to be one of a facilitator or coach or counselor. I think communicators should be in the hotspot. They need to be building partnerships—that doesn't always happen—with the human resources folks, with the finance people, with the legal people, and most importantly, with the information technology people.

Often when electronic communication is being considered, the group that gets involved early on and seems to be the natural group to go to is the information technology group or the management information system group. And the communicators aren't always included in that. And while the IT folks, of course, know the technical side of it, they might not know the communications side of it, and particularly the impact on the culture. That's the partnership the communicator needs to generate, and bring their skills forward.

Q: *Presuming there's going to be more electronic communications, what will this do to the organization?*

ALLEN: I hope not more anarchy. I think probably less rigidity. If you think about that shift—the core image of change from the traditional organizational chart to the neural structure—it's obviously more oriented towards teamwork, more of a relationship in which trust is very important. You trust people with information, as opposed to not trusting them and withholding information until they prove themselves or work high enough up the hierarchy so they can get it. It's a different mindset.

In that neural structure probably the CEO needs to be in the center, making sure that all the actions of the organization are supporting its purposes. But frankly, it probably becomes more challenging to do that.

Q: Could you comment on the evolving manager–employee relationship?

ALLEN: Probably more like a partnership. I suspect organizations that will be successful in this new environment will have to be participatory organizations rather than authoritarian organizations and that the manager will have to find ways to evoke that. I think that employees are going to be expecting that.

Q: What should IABC members be doing to catch up or train for the future?

ALLEN: It all centers on their knowledge. That's what we've seen in our studies, that no matter what the era is, the level of excellence of communication in an organization depends on the knowledge of the top communicator. So that person needs to, in this instance, talk about electronic communication, have a direct experience of what it's like to communicate electronically. You can learn a certain amount about it by reading, but the irony of that is that you're not engaged in the technology. You need to do it. Either e-mailing your mum in Vancouver—to get a sense of the potency of the media. And what it's like. The first step is to get engaged yourself. You need only to know so much about the technical side. You just need to know enough to understand applications and be able to generate new applications. That's the exciting part for communicators, who tend to be very creative people. When they get involved in the technology, they'll be able to think of new applications and shape those applications with their understanding of communications principles in the background.

Bibliography

Adweek Magazines. *Marketer's Guide to Media*. Spring/Summer 94.

Amour, N.L. The beginning of stress reduction: Creating a code of conduct for how team members treat each other. *Public Personnel Management* 24(2):127–132, 1995.

Andrews, P.H. and Baird, J.E. *Communication for Business and the Professionals*. Dubuque, IA: William C. Brown, 1986.

Angell, D. and Heslop, B. *The Internet Business Companion*. Reading, MA: Addison-Wesley, 1994.

Archea, J. The place of architectural factors in behavioral theories of privacy. *Journal of Social Issues* 33:16–137, 1977.

Arthur, M.B. Career theory in a dynamic context. In *Career Development: Theory & Practice*. D.H. Montross and C.J. Shinkman, eds. Springfield, IL: Charles C. Thomas, 1992, pp. 65–84.

Attali, J. *Millennium*. New York: Times Books (Random House), 1991.

Bacharach, S. and Aiken, M. Communication in administrative bureaucracies. *Academy of Management Journal* 20:365–377, 1977.

Bacon, T. (with Wade H. Nelson). Leading the virtual corporation. (Unpublished). October 1995.

Behrman, J.N. Cross-cultural impacts on international competitiveness. Speech given to the National Foreign Trade Council, New York, September 1, 1995.

Bennett, J.C. and Olney, R.J. Executive priorities for effective communication in an information society. *The Journal of Business Communications* 23(2):13–22, 1986.

Bennis, W.G. and Slater, P.E. *The Temporary Society*. New York: Harper & Row, 1969.

Bergman, R.E. and Moore, T.V. *Managing Interactive Video/Multimedia Projects*. Englewood Cliffs, NJ: Educational Technology Publications, 1990.

Brown, A.D. and Starkey, K. The effect of organizational culture on communication and information. *Journal of Management Studies* 31(6):807–828, 1994.

Bush, J.B. and Frohman, A.L. Communication in a "network" organization. *Organizational Dynamics* 20(2):23–36, 1991.

Carter, A.P. The economics of technological change. *Scientific American* 214(4):25–31, April 1966.

Casady, M. and Wayne, F.S. Communication skills in employment ads of major United States newspapers. *The Delta Pi Epsilon Journal* 35(2):86–99, 1993.

Chen, X.P. and Komorita, S.S. The effects of communication and commitment in a public goods social dilemma. *Organizational Behavior & Human Decision Processes* 60(3):367–386, 1994.

Curtis, D.B., Winsor, J.L., and Stephens, R.D. National preferences in business and communication education. *Communication Education* 38:6–15, 1989.

Cutlip, S.M. The challenge of the new technology for public relations practitioners. Speech delivered to the American College Public Relations Association, San Diego, California, 1973.

Czitrom, D.J. *Media and the American Mind, from Morse to McLuhan.* Chapel Hill, NC: University of North Carolina Press, 1982.

Daft, R.L. and Lengel, R.H. Information richness: A new approach to managerial behavior and organizational design. In *Research in Organizational Behavior, Vol. 6.* L.L. Cummings and B.M. Staw, eds. Greenwich, CT: JAI Press, 1984, pp. 191–233.

Daft, R.L. and Lengel, R.H. Organizational information requirements, media richness, and structural design. *Management Science* 32:554–571, 1986.

Daft, R.L., Lengel, R.H., and Trevino, L.K. Message equivocality, media selection, and manager performance: Implications for information systems. *MIS Quarterly* 11:355–366, 1987.

Dataware Technologies. *Guide to CD-ROM and Multimedia Publishing.* Dataware Technologies, March 1993.

Davidow, W.H. and Malone, M.S. *The Virtual Corporation.* New York: HarperCollins, 1992.

Diebold, J. *The Role of Business in Society.* New York: AMACOM, American Management Association, 1982.

Drucker, P.F. *The Age of Discontinuity.* New York: Harper & Row, 1969.

Drucker, P.F. *The New Realities.* New York: Harper & Row, 1989.

Drucker, P.F. *Managing the Future.* New York: American Management Association, 1994 Conference, 1994.

Drucker, P.F. *Managing in a Time of Great Change.* New York: Truman Talley Books/Dutton, 1995.

Erez, M. Interpersonal communication systems in organizations, and their relationships to cultural values, productivity, and innovation: The case of Japanese corporations. *Applied Psychology An International Review* 41:43–64, 1992.

Fabun, D. *Dynamics of Change.* Englewood Cliffs, NJ: Prentice-Hall, 1969.

Farren, C. The changing landscape of work. Unpublished white paper of Career Systems Advantage, Inc.

Fisher, A.B. America's most admired corporations. *Fortune,* March 4, 1996.

Forester, T. *High-Tech Society.* Cambridge, MA: MIT Press, 1987.

Foster, D.A. The yin and yang of management in Asia. *HR Magazine* 40(3):76–80, 1995.

Fulk, J. and Boyd, B. Emerging theories of communication in organizations. *Journal of Management* 17(2):407–446, 1991.

Gates, W.H., III. *The Road Ahead.* New York: Viking Press, 1995.

Gerstein, M.S. and Shaw, R.B. Organizational architectures for the twenty-first century. *Organizational Architecture.* San Francisco: Jossey-Bass, 1992.

Gibson, R and Lohse, D. D&B's breakup may be reverse synergy: Firm expects more profits from three-way split. *Wall Street Journal,* January 11, 1996, p. A2.

Giddens, A. *The Constitution of Society: Outline of the Theory of Structure.* Berkeley, CA: University of California Press, 1984.

Goldhaber, G.M. *Organizational Communication.* Dubuque, IA: Wm. C. Brown Publishers, 1983.

Goldmark, P.C. The new rural society. In *Papers in Communication.* Department of Communication Arts, Cornell University, Ithaca, NY, 1973.

Gudykunst, W.B. and Ting-Toomey, S. *Culture and Interpersonal Communication.* Newbury Park, CA: Sage, 1988.

Hambridge, S. Netiquette guidelines. In *Internet Engineering Task Force's Responsible Use of the Network Working Group.* (www.cnri.reston.va.us): Request for Comments 1855, October, 1995.

Harper, S.C. Business education: A view from the top. *Business Education Forum* 12(3):24–27, 1987.

Havelock, E. *Origins of Western Literacy.* Toronto: The Ontario Institute for Studies in Education, 1976.

Helvey, T.C. *Age of Information.* Englewood Cliffs, NJ: Educational Technology Publications, 1971.

Hollowell, M.L. *The Cable/Broadband Communications Book, Vol. 2, 1980–1981.* White Plains, NY: Knowledge Industry Publications, 1980.

Houston, C. and Ewing, M. Leadership in the virtual corporation. *Ways Magazine,* November 1995.

Innis, H. *The Bias of Communication.* Toronto: University of Toronto Press, 1951.

Institute of Life Insurance, Trend Analysis Program 12, New York.

Intranets revolutionize how companies operate—and communicate. *Ragan's Intranet Report,* June 1, 1996, pp.1–2.

Jensen, B. New power, real power through behavior change. *National Productivity Review* 14(3):1–8, 1995.

Johnson, D.J. Approaches to organizational structure. *Journal of Business Research* 25(2):99–113, 1992a.

Johnson, D.J. Technological and spatial factors related to organizational communication structure. *Journal of Managerial Issues* 4(2):190–209, 1992b.

Jones, J.W., Saunders, C., and McLeod, R. Information media and source patterns across management levels: A pilot study. *Journal of Management Information Systems* 5:71–84, 1988–89.

Kanter, R.M. The new managerial work. *Harvard Business Review,* 67(6):88, 91–92, 1989.

Kanter, R.M, Stein, B.A., and Jick, T.D. *The Challenge of Organizational Change: How Companies Experience It and Leaders Guide It.* New York: The Free Press, 1992.

Lakewood Research. *Training.* 1995 Industry Report. Minneapolis, MN: Lakewood Research, October.

Lee, D.M. Social ties, task-related communication and first job performance of young engineers. *Journal of Engineering & Technology Management* 11(3–4):203–228, 1994.

Lee, R.J. Getting things done in changing organizations. In *Handbook of Organizational Consultation.* R.T. Golembiewski, ed. New York: Marcel Dekker, 1993.

Lee, R.T. and Ashford, B.E. Work-unit structure and processes and job-related stressors as predictors of managerial burn-out. *Journal of Applied Psychology* 21(22):1831–1847, 1991.

Levinson, H. Why behemoths fall: Psychological roots of corporate failure. *American Psychologist* 49(5):428–436, 1994.

Levinson, N.S. and Asahi, M. Cross-national alliances and inter-organizational learning. *Organizational Dynamics* 24(2):50–62, 1995.

Lewis, P.H. Trying to find gold with the Internet. *New York Times,* January 3, 1995, p. C15.

Lohr, S. Big companies cloud recovery by cutting jobs. *New York Times,* December 17, 1992.

Malone, T.W. and Rockart, J.F. Computers, networks and the corporation. *Scientific American,* September 1991.

Marlow, E. *Managing Corporate Media.* White Plains, NY: Knowledge Industry Publications, 1989.

Marlow, E. *Corporate Television Programming.* White Plains, NY: Knowledge Industry Publications, 1992.

Marlow, E. *Winners! Producing Effective Electronic Media.* Belmont, CA: Wadsworth, 1994.

Marlow, E. and Secunda, E. *Shifting Time and Space: The Story of Videotape.* New York: Praeger, 1991.

Marshak, R.J. Managing the metaphors of change. *Organizational Dynamics* 22(1):44–56, 1993.

Marting, E., Finley, R., and Ward, A., eds. *Effective Communication on the Job.* New York: American Management Association, rev. ed., 1963.

Matthes, K. Television catches employees' eyes. *Personnel Magazine,* May 1991.

McLuhan, M. *Understanding Media: The Extensions of Man.* New York: McGraw-Hill, 1964.

Meyrowitz, J. *No Sense of Place.* New York: Oxford University Press, 1985.

Microsoft Corporation. *Multimedia Publishing and Microsoft Multimedia,* Viewer Publishing Toolkit Version 2.0, February 1993.

Miller, C. and Aeppel, T. BMW zooms ahead of Mercedes-Benz in world-wide sales for the first time. *Wall Street Journal,* January 29, 1993, p. B1.

Miller, R. Going inside with the Internet. *IABC Communication World,* November 1995.

Nadler, D.A., Gerstein, M.S., and Shaw, R.B. *Organizational Architecture: Designs for Changing Organizations.* San Francisco: Jossey-Bass, 1992.

National Association of Broadcasters. *User's Guide,* Washington, DC, 1994.

National Cable Television Association. *Cable Television Developments.* Washington, D.C.: National Cable Television Association, Spring 1996.

Nemee, R. Compassion is OK in the business world. *Communication World* 12(5):20–22, 1995.

Nicolini, D. and Meznar, M.B. The social construction of organizational learning: Conceptual and practical issues in the field. *Human Relations* 48(7):727–746, 1995.

Noer, D.M. *Healing the Wounds: Overcoming the Trauma of Layoffs and Revitalizing Downsized Organizations.* San Francisco: Jossey-Bass, 1993.

Orlikowski, W.J. and Yates, J. Genre repertoire: The structuring of communicative practices in organizations. *Administrative Science Quarterly* 39:541–574, 1994.

Palmer, I. and Lundberg, C.C. Metaphors of hospitality organizations: An exploratory study. *Cornell Hotel & Restaurant Administrative Quarterly* 36(3):80–85, 1995.

Peters, T.J. *Liberation Management: Necessary Disorganization for the Nanosecond Nineties.* New York: Knopf, 1992.

Phillips, N. and Brown, J.L. Analysing communication in and around organizations: A critical hermeneutic approach. *Academy of Management Journal* 26(6):1547–1576, 1993.

Porter, L.W. and McKibbin, L.E. *Management Education and Development: Drift or Thrust into the 21st Century?* New York: McGraw-Hill, 1988.

Quintanilla, C. More top executives are hitting the road. *Wall Street Journal* Travel, January 12, 1995, p. B1.

Ready, D. and Gouillart, F.J. (1994). Champions of change: A global report on leading business transformation. Dr. Douglas Ready, Executive Director, International Consortium for Executive Development Research and Gemini Consulting.

Reeves, T. and Harmon, S. What's in a name—hypermedia. *Interact, the Journal of the International Interactive Communications Society,* fall 1991.

Rheingold, H. *Virtual Reality.* New York: Touchstone Books, Simon & Schuster, 1991.

Rice, R.E. and Shook, D.E. Voice messaging, coordination, and communication. In *Intellectual Technology: Social and Technological Foundations of Cooperative Work.* R.K. Galegher and C. Egido, eds. Hillsdale, NJ: Erlbaum, 1989.

Robinson, S.L. and Rousseau, D.M. Violating the psychological contract: Not the exception, but the norm. *Journal of Organizational Behavior* 15(3):245–259, 1994.

Roebuck, D.B., Sightler, K.W., and Brush, C.C. Organizational size, copay type, and position effects on the perceived importance of oral and written communication skills. *Journal of Managerial Issues* 7(1):99–115, 1995.

Rogers, E.M. *Communication Technology: The New Media in Society.* New York: The Free Press, 1986.

Rutten, P., Bayers, A.F., and Maloni, K. *Netguide.* New York: Michael Wolff & Company, 1994.

Samuelson, R.J. *The Good Life and its Discontents: The American Dream in the Age of Entitlement 1945–1995.* New York: Times Books, 1995.

Sanders, L. Future shop. In *Business Communication: Concepts and Applications in an Electronic Age,* 5th ed. R.H. Hudson and B.J. Selzer, eds. Los Angeles, CA: Roxbury Publishing, 1994.

Schall, M.S. A communication-rules approach to organizational culture. *Administrative Science Quarterly* 28:557–581, 1983.

Schubin, M. An overview and history of video disc technologies. In *Video Discs, The Technology, the Applications and the Future.* Sigel et al., eds. White Plains, NY: Knowledge Industry Publications, 1980.

Scudder, J.N. and Guinan, P.J. Communication competencies as discriminators of superiors' ratings of employee performance. *The Journal of Business Communication* 26(3):217–229, 1989.

Scully, J.P. People: The imperfect communicators. *Quality Progress* 28(4):37–39, 1995.

Smith, L.F. *Perspectives on Radio & Television.* New York: Harper & Row, 1985.

Snyder, R.A. and Morris, J.H. Organization communication and performance. *Journal of Applied Psychology* 69(3):461–465, 1984.

Stewart, T.A. Looking out for number 1: A complete guide to your career. *Fortune*, January 15, 1996, p. 33.

Stokes, J.T. *The Business of Nonbroadcast Television.* White Plains, NY: Knowledge Industry Publications, 1988.

Stryker, S. and Stratham, A. (1985). Symbolic interaction and role theory. In *New Handbook of Social Psychology.* Lindzey, G. and Aronson, E., eds. 1:311–378. New York: Random House.

Tesler, L.G. Network computing in the 1990s. *Scientific American*, September 1991, pp. 86–93.

Theus, K.T. Communication in a power vacuum: Sense-making and enactment during crisis-induced departures. *Human Resource Management* 34(1):27–49, 1995.

Toffler, A. *Future Shock.* New York: Random House, 1970.

Tribus, M. and McIrvine, E.C. Energy and information. *Scientific American*, September 1971.

Troy, K. Change management: Communication's pivotal role. New York: The Conference Board Report Number 1122–95-RR, 1995.

Tuchi, C.L. and Lojo, M.P. Social comparisons and cooperative R&D ventures: The double-edge sword of communication. *Journal of Engineering & Technology Management* 11(3–4):187–202, 1994.

Ulrich, D., Glinow, M.A., and Jick, T. High-impact learning: Building and diffusing learning capability. *Organizational Dynamics* 22(2):52–66, 1993.

Urry, J. Social relations, space, and time. In *Social Relations and Spatial Structures.* D. Gregory and J. Urry, eds. Hong Kong: MacMillan, 1985.

Vaill, P. *Managing as a Performing Art.* San Francisco: Jossey-Bass, 1989.

Venn, G. *Man, Education, and Manpower.* American Association of School Administration. Washington, DC, 1970.

Weick, K.E. Theorizing about organizational communication. In *Handbook of Organizational Communication.* F.M. Jablin, L.L. Putnam, K.H. Roberts, and L.W. Porter, eds. Newbury Park, CA: Sage, 1987, pp. 97–122.

Wiley, J.B. *Communication for Modern Management.* Elmhurst, IL: The Business Press, 1966.

Winston, B. *Misunderstanding Media.* Cambridge, MA: Harvard University Press, 1986.

Young, M. and Post, J.E. Managing to communicate, communicating to manage: How leading companies communicate with employees. *Organizational Dynamics* 22(1):31–43, 1993.

Zajas, J. A group process assessment for interpersonal growth, communications, and managerial development. *International Journal of Management* 11(3):773–777, 1994.

Index

Eugene Marlow, Ph.D. (emabb@cunyvm.cuny.edu) has been involved with the strategic application of print and electronic media for over 30 years. He has consulted to dozens of organizations in the media, technology, healthcare, consumer products, and non-profit sectors. He teaches graduate and undergraduate courses in electronic journalism and business communications at Bernard M. Baruch College (City University of New York).

Dr. Marlow is the author of numerous books, including *Web Visions: An Inside Look at Successful Business Strategies on the Net* (Van Nostrand Reinhold, 1996), *Electronic Public Relations* (Wadsworth Publishing, 1996), *Winners! Producing Effective Electronic Media* (Wadsworth, 1994), and *Managing Corporate Media, 2nd Edition* (Knowledge Industry Publications, 1989).

Patricia O' Connor Wilson, MBA (wilsonpo@leaders.ccl.org) works for the Center for Creative Leadership (CCL), an international non-profit educational institution devoted to behavioral science research, executive development, and leadership education. Her role at CCL focuses on assessing the leadership development needs of client organizations, providing liaison services between clients and Center resources which best respond to those needs, and teams training.

Ms. Wilson has conducted research in the areas of managerial effectiveness, self-efficacy, and entrepreneurialism. Other areas of interest include large systems strategic change, high performing teams, and development systems.

*For Product Safety Concerns and Information please contact
our EU representative GPSR@taylorandfrancis.com Taylor & Francis
Verlag GmbH, Kaufingerstraße 24, 80331 München, Germany*

T - #0085 - 230425 - C0 - 229/152/11 - PB - 9780750697460 - Gloss Lamination